PHILIPSON

a biography of
Sir Robin Philipson

W. GORDON SMITH

ATELIER BOOKS
Edinburgh

FIRST PUBLISHED 1995 BY
ATELIER BOOKS
4 DUNDAS STREET • EDINBURGH EH3 6HZ
TEXT © COPYRIGHT W. GORDON SMITH, 1995
ISBN 1873 830 033

Production and publishing consultant Paul Harris
Printed in Slovenia by Gorenjski Tisk

The Publisher thanks Lady Diana Philipson
for Kind Permission to use all photographs
of Sir Robin's Work

ACKNOWLEDGEMENTS

IN ANY ENTERPRISE OF THIS COMPLEXITY THERE ARE, INEVITABLY, MANY debts to pay. Phyllis Gwilliam, Robin's twin sister, filled out her brother's early life for me and spurred me on with constant encouragement. Jack Firth, a meticulous keeper of records and old friend of Robin's, proffered his personal archive with generosity and comradely good will. Scotland has cause to be grateful for his unselfish interest in brother artists.

It will be evident from their many contributions to my text that colleagues, friends and former students held Robin Philipson, artist and man, in special regard. They needed no coaxing to say so. Four books have been of considerable value to me: Maurice Lindsay's monograph on Philipson (Edinburgh University Press, 1976); William Hardie's "Scottish Painting, 1837 to the Present" (Studio Vista, 1990); Edward Gage's "The Eye in the Wind" (Collins, 1977), and Duncan Macmillan's "Scottish Art 1460–1990" (Mainstream, 1990). I am indebted to them.

All the photographs in the book are, so far as I could ascertain, the work of Jack Firth, Bill Brady and Antonia Reeve. I thank them and the owners of the paintings.

Throughout his life Robin, having said all he wanted to say with his brushes, found it difficult to find titles for his paintings. Indeed, some remained orphans, others were given more than one name at different times, and a great many found themselves sharing versions of generic titles – Arena, Women and Men Observed, Humankind, Cockfight, Rose Window, and several others. Specific titles have been used only when their provenance seemed certain.

My wife and professional partner Jay Gordonsmith was with me when we made a film about Robin Philipson in 1971 – indeed, it would not have happened without her – and this book is testament to her dedicated support and sustenance.

FOREWORD

by John Bellany

EARLY SKIRMISH

THIS IS A PARABLE ABOUT AUDACITY, TOLERANCE AND GENEROSITY OF spirit. IN 1963 I was elected president of the sketch club at Edinburgh College of Art, an organisation outwith staff control. We could put on our own exhibitions in the college of work done at home or in our studios and get outside people to do a crit. I had this brainwave. We would have a drawing competition between students and staff and judged by an outsider. Two teams of five, like football, competing in the college sculpture court. A referee in attendance to judge a grand event. Two of the staff immediately agreed to take part. The audacity of the idea spread like wildfire. Unfortunately it reached Robin's ears. I was hauled straight to his room and given the telling-off of the century. I was offending the professional standards of his staff and if Gillies, then the principal, got to hear of it I would be marching out the front gate, never to return. However, as was his way, after Robin delivered the row he just laughed his head off at my audacity.

AWOL IN 1964

At the start of my fourth year Robin hauled me up to his room for being AWOL during the first three days of term. I had been spending my grant on fun and games. He had just returned from teaching art at summer school in Boulder, Colorado, and was full of it. The conservative blue smock had been replaced with a new American job and bright plimsolls. His perpetual bow tie had given way to a jazzy cravat. Robin usually started off with a ponderous speech, then a tirade, then a rant. He told me how wonderful the American art school system was, how students selected staff, and how the staff waited in the wings to see if their auditions had persuaded the students to select them. I was then told how easy it was to be a big fish in a small Edinburgh pond, not to get carried away, watch my step and not get too big for my boots. He calmed down. "You must keep your own identity. You must never lose sight of your own vision, however grand or modest it might be. You think the world's out there. It's actually here, the world we're living in. Make the most of every minute you have here. I'll keep my beady eye on you to see you don't go off the straight and narrow." He had wanted to give me a row but let me see another side of him. I was forced to ask, as I was being shown the door, "so you think it's better in Edinburgh than America?" He just gave me a knowing smile and closed the door behind me.

Thirst was heavy at that period. From Port Seton one Saturday morning I phoned him at his home to say hello. I was up on a visit from London. Obviously the call came out of the blue, but I was welcomed for lunch. I arrived at his posh house and met Diana and their son Jasper. A bottle of slivowitz appeared. He was saving it for a very special occasion. Lady Diana said, "so you're honoured." But not nearly so honoured as when I was shown into the drawingroom and there in pride of place on the main wall was an early 6'x7' painting I had given him in 1967. I was totally surprised and flabbergasted. Robin said they loved living with it and had the walls painted a special bright blue to suit the picture. The other paintings, mostly small oils and watercolours by his close friends and colleagues in the Scottish art scene seemed to look on in astonishment at the big Bellany. After lunch I did a drawing of Jasper, as a present. Jasper returned the compliment. Then I drew his father and handed him pencil and paper, inviting him to immortalise me. He did a lovely study which I have hanging in my drawingroom. Robin had a great sense of occasion and a self-effacing sense of fun.

THE SCOTTISH DELACROIX

Helen and I visited Robin in Chalmers Hospital, opposite the art college. I was the bane of his life for two decades, yet, ill as he was, he still had that sparkle and twinkle in his eyes. We reflected on countless memories of the place across the road, and the great joy we all had there. I had taken him a Rembrandt book as a present and said: "Robin, can't you see what the man on the front of this book is saying. He is telling the Scottish Delacroix (my name for him) to keep well and get painting again." Within three weeks he did another Lazarus and was back at the brushes. Big six-foot paintings. Nothing stopped him painting.

"The Visit – Night"

"Women Observed"

PREFACE

For over a year we talked about this book before February 1992, when the first of many Monday-night recording sessions began at Robin's home at Crawfurd Road, Edinburgh. Each of us, without acknowledging it, heard "time's wingèd chariot hurrying near." Once again he was very ill. Chemotherapy was now trying to keep at bay the disease which had assaulted him, off and on for 20 years, and which surgery had failed to eradicate. The drugs nauseated him. All liquid tasted of iron filings. Yet, like the good host he never failed to be, a decent bottle of wine stood uncorked for me, warming by a blazing fire.

His voice creaked and squeaked and sometimes groaned as the spools of tape spun on. He delved deep to remember things, found something else on the way, laughed at himself, recalled pain as well as pleasure, remembered friends and their kindnesses, spoke of his work, always his work, from the vast altarpieces that once crowded his college studio to the pastels he was now drawing daily on his knee because he no longer had enough strength to stand at the easel. One moment he was hearing the Naga tribesmen of Burma singing Welsh hymns they had learned from Christian missionaries; the next he saw his mother baking and testing the heat of her oven with the back of her hand. He was running from a caravan at Colinton to catch the tram to college, acting the daft laddie with Alan Davie, touring the Queen round the RSA, hammering an old banger all the way to France to catch a sunny picture.

Each week he grew more feeble. More than once, with my heart sinking, I suggested we should stop. He insisted that we should go on – if I could stand it, so could he. Without food, sipping only liquid concoctions that garred him grue, he had no physical resources, and soon he could no longer hang on to the thread of a single thought and grasped, with a sudden spurt of energy, at some fresh tendril of memory. It was as if his mind was already divided up like one of his more complex canvases, a montage of images conjured out of a tumbled mass, separate yet connected by horizontal and vertical bars of rainbow, advancing and receding, veiled in semi-transparent gauze or suddenly revealed in a trumpeting choir of colour.

And I wondered if – behind the assured public figure, the master of many ceremonies, the dapper wit, the articulate erudite charmer – behind the bright intelligence of the fit and energetic man, was this always how a darting, wondering, incandescent mind had stoked the fires and possessed the life and work of the artist Robin Philipson.

12   PHILIPSON

TUESDAY, MAY 26, 1992

Throughout my whole life, during every moment I have lived, the world has gradually been taking on light and fire for me, until it has come to envelop me in one mass of luminosity, glowing from within… the purple flush of matter imperceptibly fading into the gold of spirit, to be lost finally in the incandescence of a personal universe.

Tielhard de Chardin

Quoted by Robin Philipson in the catalogue of his Bruton Gallery exhibition *Zigzag of Time* in 1991

News of his death at the Royal Infirmary of Edinburgh, came as a profound shock but no surprise. He had held on so often, clung to life with such ferocity, scrambled back to work so restored and eager, over the years he seemed to have become indestructible. But those who knew him in the last months and saw shadow replace substance, heard the timbre seep out of his voice and watched strength ebb from his body, felt in their hearts that this time he was slipping away.

The public funeral, at the heart of the crossroads they call Edinburgh's Holy Corner, was uplifting and splendid. Sunlight shafted over the huge assembly. Singing and sweet music challenged solemnity.

The Very Reverend Gilleasbuig Macmillan, Minister of St Giles' Cathedral, chaplain to the Royal Scottish Academy, had crossed the town to speak brave words about a friend.

Another friend, the actor Tom Fleming, used Kipling's *When Earth's Last Picture is Painted* to make us smile, and perhaps recognise someone we had known, with the lines:

> *And those that were good shall be happy:*
> *they shall sit in a golden chair;*
> *They shall splash at a ten-league canvas*
> *with brushes of comets' hair.*

Sir Robin Philipson, PPRSA RA HRA RSW RGI D.(Univ) LL.D FRSE HRIAS RCAA HRHA DA(Edin). His titles, degrees and decorations read like battle honours, this railwayman's son from Broughton-in-Furness, then Gretna, before he began the long process of becoming a Scotsman – schoolboy at Dumfries, student at Edinburgh College of Art, officer in the King's Own Scottish Borderers, lecturer then head of the school of drawing and painting at ECA, academican in Edinburgh, London and Dublin, president of the Royal Scottish Academy, awarded doctorates and gongs and scrolls and scholarships.

Yet an establishment figure who never quite joined. A compulsive working artist who never lost his terror of an empty canvas. A warm, curiously shy, soft-hearted man with abundant social graces and the gift of friendship.

It is difficult to know who got the best of him. His family and intimate friends, of course. His pals, students and colleagues during 45 years at the college he called "a damn great canvas." The members of the Academy he served with such idiosyncratic flair and affection. The many hundreds of people who treasure the Philipson on their walls and feel the surge of his ardent spirit. The citizens of Edinburgh whose social scene was decorated by his kenspeckle figure. The folk who did him small services and have cause to remember his kindness. They all got something; he was very generous with himself.

For such a serious man, whose blazing honesty and fierce intelligence stoked the turbulent energies of his creative life, he was incurably romantic. The nattiest of dressers, a bearer of bouquets, he could put himself on parade. Quick to laugh, even quicker to generate laughter, his eyes dancing with mischief.

Philipson the painter, for he wanted to be nothing else, secured his place in twentieth-century Scottish art 30 years before when his fighting cocks, savage yet decorative traumas of colour and movement, became the first of many thematic subjects which would run through his paintings like insistent tunes. Rose windows glowing like lava. The threnody of the 1914–18 war to end all wars. Cathedral interiors wrought, it seemed, out of Inca gold. The haunting sexual polarity of black girl and white boy. The sea in a tumult. All those odalisques and houris lounging in erotic dalliance. Sinister pye dogs, elegant horses and zebras, and emblematic poppies waving flags at the light.

A romantic expressionist, if we must have a label, a Colourist in Edinburgh's *belle peinture* tradition, and a restless, constantly questing innovator. He was a superb technician, a consummate craftsman, and in watercolour a master of that medium's fugitive delicacies.

Only a few weeks before going into hospital for the last time he had to abandon painting because he could no longer stand at the easel. So he contented himself, for as long as he could, working at home with the rich intensity of pastel, looking for "that sleeping surprise," as he called it – the essence of his art – which he caught so often on the wing.

MARTIN BAILLIE – Only time can bring a final appraisal of his achievement, but what can be said is that Robin Philipson developed the Scottish Colourist tradition by looking beyond the borders of Scottish painting.

BARBARA BALMER – He was an exemplary President of the RSA. Members will recall that he was always present at one's private view, often held on precious Saturday mornings. A man of great style reflected both in his person and his work.

LILIAN BROWSE – All those who knew Robin – and who in the Scottish arts scene did not? – will share the same sense of loss as I feel so deeply, for not only was he one of Scotland's most distinguished painters, he was also a life-enhancer.

FRANCIS CONVERY – In my first year at Edinburgh (1979) we were spoken to by the three Heads of School; Painting, Sculpture and Design. I don't remember all that Robin said, but remember clearly his conclusion: "To be an artist and painter is the greatest thing you could ever be, the most honourable way to use your life"… That was good enough for me.

DAVID EVANS – I first met Robin in the summer of 1965, when I came up from London to be interviewed for a teaching job at ECA. I remember being a little in awe, in my early teaching days, of this elegantly-dressed man. I have marvellous affectionate memories of a kind, hospitable, eager, enthusiastic, stimulating and lovely man.

IAN FLEMING – He was, in my opinion, arguably the outstanding Scottish artist in this century. He was also a distinguished President of the RSA – articulate and always commanding attention – a man without peer

JACK KNOX – In his painting he was a superb craftsman in complete command of his language, yet constantly probing and questioning his art. He will be remembered by many for his generous praise, and particularly for his enthusiastic support of young artists.

JOHN BUSBY – His was a creative force always there in the background – an influence and an inspiration in one's own struggle to find an individual voice as an artist. One of the best times, if not THE best era of ECA.

DAVID MICHIE – The act of painting seemed to be for Robin a kind of ritual where the themes of his interest were summoned to sit at his table and join a dialogue, to become the focal point of his painting, and to assist in their creation.

JAMES MORRISON – I knew him best as President of the RSA and I reckon in my time he was by far the best. He brought to the job a dignity, grace and elegance wholly appropriate to the position, and continued to be – despite the heavy duties – a vigorous, significant painter.

ALBERTO MORROCCO – He was a man of great kindness, generosity and friendliness. I cannot remember his ever maligning or talking down any other artist of our mutual acquaintance – and that must be considered pretty unique in the world of art. He certainly is one of the finest painters that Scotland has produced.

GUY PEPLOE – I believe Robin Philipson was a man of immense intelligence and integrity. I remember him as a great man who made you feel equal, who listened, and whose words you remembered.

JUNE REDFERN – Robin was Head of Painting when I was a student. In 1973 someone made a wee film in homage to him. We all stood, in our platform Biba boots, on Arthur's Seat, gathered together in the shape of a large bow tie, holding flash cards to represent the spots, and singing, "When the Red Red Robin comes bob-bob-bobbing along…" He loved it, of course. I was privileged. He was a one-off.

ROGER BILLCLIFFE – His contribution to painting in Scotland, his commitment to art education here and to the course steered by the Royal Scottish Academy, has all seemed to confirm his Scottishness, his role in a definable tradition of Scottish painting which can be traced back to the eighteenth century and which we like to think is very much alive today. But Robin Philipson is not a Scot, and the more I look at his painting the less Scottish I find it. Only on rare occasions, and in the hands of very few painters, has Scottish painting been concerned with other than the here and now. Scots have excelled as still-life and landscape painters; as portraitists they have few equals when they set their minds to it. Their art has, on the whole been reactive. It is usually concerned with a subject which presents itself to the artist, whether in the studio or outdoors, but it has its roots in reality. It is a physical and mental response to a visual stimulation which excites the application of paint, the choice of colour, the painterly gesture… But few painters in Scotland choose to call upon their own imagination to produce work which tests our preconception of pictorial design, combined with the assured, yet often experimental, technique that we encounter in the works of Robin Philipson.

JUDITH BUMPUS – If his heart lay in Scotland, Philipson made a point of keeping a foot in London. Less appreciated south of the Border than he deserved to be, he had many English admirers nevertheless, and was held by those who knew him in as deep affection as he was by Scottish contemporaries. At once highly intelligent and elusively romantic, his song – or perhaps I should say his message to us – was orchestrated with a brilliant handling of colour, tone and surface texture. There was a vitality and immediacy about all his work that belied the long reflection that produced it.

CHAPTER ONE

ROBERT JAMES PHILIPSON AND HIS TWIN SISTER PHYLLIS WERE BORN ON December 17, 1916 in a fine house standing on its own, with a driveway, garden, orchard and surrounded by fields at Broughton Mills, near Lake Coniston in Cumbria. Their father, James, was a railwayman – stationmaster as well as porter and ticket collector – in sole charge of the tiny Broughton Mills halt. Their mother, Agnes Postlethwaite, had been a farmer's widow in her early 30s and the mother of three young children when James married her. The twins were born in the second year of the new marriage; the Philipsons went on to have another daughter and son.

In this happy household of seven children Robert James was never called anything else but Robin – his mother's choice of name from the start, but he had been christened Robert in honour of his father's brother. The twins enjoyed a special bond that lasted 75 years. Phyllis remembers being told that her mother thought she had given birth to two "odd ones" – a girl who would have nothing to do with dolls and a boy who preferred paper and pencil to any kind of toy. They had reached the age of six before they stopped walking everywhere hand-in-hand. Chatting one day to the local doctor Mrs Philipson wondered aloud about this behaviour, but was told not to worry, "they probably held hands in the womb."

Robin remembered a gentle childhood, with a mother who was artistic in many simple ways – "a creative seamstress, cook and baker, and a clever gardener." He hunted about in his mind for a more precise definition… *"she built one's imagination, that's it, in so many ways"* – by her gift of storytelling and her encouragement, bordering on adulation, of his childish drawing. From the earliest days he could remember, when she was asked, "what's he going to be?" his mother's reply was, "I think he's going to be an artist." Looking back he believed it really was just as simple as that, as if it had been ordained – not by some omnipotent deity, but by the evidence of his natural ability and single-minded enthusiasm. And didn't he have strange tastes for a young lad? When he was given money to buy sweets and always chose fruit gums it was assumed he liked the variety of flavours; when asked, however, he talked only about how their bright clear colours gleamed when he held them up to the light.

Baking days were special – "washdays were lousy." He sat at his mother's feet on the kitchen floor and copied pictures from newspapers and magazines. "Copying is irrevocably bad for you, but what else can you draw when you're only five or six?" All he remembered about that time was a cocoon of cosiness, the warmth of an open stove, tantalising baking smells, his mother's plump busy arms kneading dough, and the way she tested the heat of the oven with the back of her hand. Of a carefree boyhood out of doors all he could recall was chasing chickens.

For reasons known only to himself the adult man never spoke about being a boy soprano in the church choir. He sang a lot about the house, casually rehearsing a forthcoming solo or just enjoying himself. Music meant much to him. Early piano lessons gave him a good grounding and throughout his life he played for his own pleasure, enjoyed concerts, and in the studio – as many artists do – he played recorded music constantly, using it as stimulant and tranquilliser, inspiration and solace.

from "Arena" series

James Philipson was a respectable, responsible man of quick intelligence whose education had been cut short, by family circumstances, much too soon. Throughout his life he sublimated an inner compulsion similar to the one that drove his son to become an artist; in his case the enthusiasm was for the theory and practise of medicine – he would have given anything to have become a doctor. Instead he studied first-aid. In his day railway staff were expected to be able to administer rudimentary treatment in emergencies. He led teams of colleagues who won prizes for bandaging and resuscitating victims of mock rail disasters. Unusually for a working man in the years between the wars, when dressing for any small social event, he always wore a bow tie. His son sported them, often flamboyantly, all his adult life. Robin also inherited his father's almost courtly manners, distinguished by a polite bob or tilt of the head when being introduced to a stranger.

The railway job moved the family about Cumbria when the children were young. The twins were bright at their primary schools. Robin's constant drawing led inevitably to his first experiments with colour. He learned to use crayons – sticks of stiff and rather dull wax rather than the vibrant soft pastels he would master much later in life – and by the time he was 11 or 12 he was encouraged by some now-forgotten influence to make a small window of stained glass which was installed in Whitehaven school. Many years later, when Phyllis came home to be married, she remembers catching the glint of it from the roadside.

London & North Eastern Railways promoted James Philipson and moved him to Gretna. The twins, aged 14, became boarders at Dumfries Academy, the imposing red sandstone edifice on a bank of the Nith, which boasted J M Barrie as a former pupil. Robin was not entirely happy. Some of the staff gave him a hard time – "they must have wondered what this funny animal was going to turn out to be, especially since the animal arrived without assets, without a distinction in anything, not even a prize for art." He had been favoured in his Cumbrian school, "a kind of special guy," and at Dumfries he found himself treated "as an also ran – even less than an also ran." But not entirely. His natural artistic gifts, the hand-and-eye facility which he had exercised even at primary school, encouraged him to make cut-out silhouette portraits, small commissions which augmented his pocket money.

Fate, in the person of a man called Jock Ramsay, also proffered a benign hand. Throughout Scotland in the 1930s art joined physical education, music and other esoteric subjects at the fagend of the average school curriculum. Classics, mathematics and science offered prospects of advancement in life – almost everything else was regarded as recreation. Dumfries might have been no different if it had not been for Ramsay. He was not only an enthusiastic teacher of art, but so highly regarded as an educator that he was also the school's deputy principal.

In 1978, while thanking the University of Aberdeen for bestowing on him an honorary LLD, Philipson jocularly suggested, as he often did, that school had taught him nothing of consequence. The remark was intended as a self-denigrating aside, but it was reported widely enough for it to reach the ears of Ramsay's widow, who, knowing the part that her husband had played in Philipson's early development, made it known to him that she was disappointed and hurt. Philipson quickly repaired the damage. He reminded her of a happy and poignant occasion when he had declared his debt to her husband. When the date for Ramsay's formal retiral was decided in 1966 it happened to coincide with his birthday. The school asked him to choose a present to mark that extra-special day. "Anything at all?" he asked. "Whatever you would like," he was told. He thought for a moment then said: "Ask Robin Philipson to come and present the prizes on my last day. I never gave him a prize for art and I had better make it up to him now."

Philipson acknowledged that Ramsay taught him many tangible things about art and opened his mind to some of its intangibles. Above all Ramsay insisted that he would have to take art seriously. "He made me see that it had to be that way or nothing at all. It was an important lesson which took a while to implant but never left me." He remembered his teacher as a very splendid man – "a nice, gentle man who loved cricket, thank God, and so did I." Apart from the occasional smack of willow on leather Philipson took no part in school sport. "I was hopeless." But it was his habit to affect that self-mocking diffidence about many things, making the kind of dismissive statement that was misunderstood at Aberdeen.

Phyllis, remembering their time at Dumfries Academy, says he was a conscientious scholar, good at everything except mathematics. Robin insisted that his problem subject was English. Phyllis maintains that he was mistaken. No matter the subject, his difficulties with one or other of these essential passports to progress posed a serious problem when he approached the Higher Leaving Certificate examinations. He would need good passes in a group of subjects, including English and maths, in order to gain entry to an art college. Robin's versions of the drama began with "we better get the record clear: it took me three shots, and I thought I was on the threshold of failing my Highers. Damned near gave me a nervous breakdown. I had applied to Edinburgh College of Art and Glasgow School of Art. I was on tenterhooks. Then a Scottish minister in the township of Gretna – we were not of his parish – having heard of my predicament, made an appeal on my behalf in the right quarter.

"The Inspector of Schools arrived one day and, in an empty classroom, asked me to talk back to him the answers to his questions. We had been speaking for only about five minutes when he said 'Right, that's it!' A most unusual thing, and for me, a miracle. I've been aware, in a kind of terrified way, that I've enjoyed speaking ever since, but I've had to work very hard at it. I hate writing. I never write except under duress."

Philipson got his Highers and gained entrance to Edinburgh College of Art in 1936. He was to be there, with the exception of his war service years, until 1982.

ROBIN PHILIPSON (about our recorded interviews) – I wouldn't want to spend too much time summing up, but I'd like to spend a lot of time being irritated. I've always been worn out by people who irritate me.

You come into Scotland at the age of 14 or 15 from England, from Cumbria, and you're on a hiding to nothing, but I've said it over and over again, and I believe it very sincerely, that if you have to graduate to becoming a Scot, 14 or 15 is a very good age at which to do it – painful, difficult, but permanent. That is what happened to me. I was very fortunate.

Going back to Dumfries all these years later for Jock Ramsay's retiral, I realised he had been such a good teacher, such an enormous enthusiast for art. He was kind about what had happened to me, my career at Edinburgh, the development of my painting. And he reminded me how he had talked to me, as a boy, about his affection for art which related abstraction to realism, so that neither of them had a positive identity, and were not entirely coherent. A lot of that stuck with me, stimulated me, and could apply to a vast amount of my work. I'm really rather terrified – in some ways and on some occasions – of coherence. It can be a damned nuisance. So you circumnavigate it, like a wolf going round a sheep – circumnavigate, and watch, and see.

An interesting thing happened at Jock's farewell party. I had a funny little Morris 8 which, full out, went about 30 miles an hour. When we reached Dumfries we checked and checked to a stupid degree that we had locked the car because it was parked outside the main building and the ceremony was in an adjacent building. When we came back to the car to go home it was full of flowers, but the doors were still locked. Wasn't that a nice little ruse on somebody's part? I know I didn't leave the key lying around, so obviously they must have gotten in and gotten out again somehow. Very nice.

At school, as I remember it, paints were frail things. We had crayons. I remember a pastel drawing of a blue saucepan done by a boy in my class, and I saw the cream lining… I thought it was the most beautiful thing I'd seen in my life. It knocked me over, so I took to doing some pastels with him. Watercolour was beyond us, really. Today I notice they use watercolour and accept whatever the children do. Well in my day you had to make it look like the thing you were painting, it had to be disciplined, the ellipses had to be ellipses, that sort of thing. A different ball game, and very innocent, with a modest amount of time allocated. Dumfries was very good. Poster colour was the great thing in those days. You couldn't go away and buy a pot of it, you had to mix it up and that was good to do. I burgeoned. I don't have any of them now, thank god. When I think of the things I did at Dumfries, they really were just terrible.

TOM LOCHHEAD (potter, schoolfriend and fellow student at Edinburgh) – We met in the art room. I'm not quite sure – I think we were 17 or maybe 18. By that time we'd asked to be allowed to drop various subjects, so we could do art all the time. I was building myself a caravan, Robin had got his Highers and did nothing but paint and draw. We had a glorious time, especially in that last summer term. They were demolishing the junior school in order to build the present academy. It was a good June. We were outside all day, sketching the men at work… Robin was always better than me. He wasn't flashy, even when we went to art college he wasn't one of those recognised immediately. There were those who had a bit more flair, but Robin was always working, always searching out. He was a terrific worker.

CHAPTER TWO

Iʀ, ᴀꜰᴛᴇʀ Gʀᴇᴛɴᴀ, Dᴜᴍꜰʀɪᴇs ᴡᴀs ʙʀɪɢʜᴛ ʟɪɢʜᴛs ᴀɴᴅ ᴍᴀʀᴋᴇᴛ-ᴛᴏᴡɴ bustle, Edinburgh's spectacular grandeur, its Jekyll and Hyde polarity of stately Georgian terraces and apalling slums, the clash of its streets and pandemonium of its pubs, the "draughty parallelograms" of its New Town and teetering tenements of the old historic capital perched over the ribbed closes and vennels of the Royal Mile, made such an impact on Philipson's young mind that he never seriously considered making his home anywhere else in the world. He might just as easily have gone to Glasgow, become absorbed in that other great city's very different culture, come under the influence of other minds, been swayed by different artistic disciplines, but to the end of his days he felt fate had been good to him. From almost his first moment in the place he knew he belonged.

Edinburgh College of Art, founded in 1908 – only a year earlier than the formal opening of Charles Rennie Mackintosh's Glasgow School of Art – had seen its students go off to one terrible war and, as Philipson walked through the doors at Lauriston Place in 1936, Europe was in political and economic ferment and the world was on the brink of another catastrophe.

As a teaching establishment ECA was still fiercely dedicated to classicism. Modern art was at least half-a-century old. The Impressionists had been succeeded by the Post-Impressionists. The Fauves and Cubists and Nabis had been and gone. Matisse and Picasso were still pushing out new frontiers of modernism, but they might have been working on the moon so far as the college was concerned, where the curriculum slavishly obeyed the diktat of the past. ECA's inherited purpose was to instil exacting standards of academic excellence, teach technical skills and the classical rules of composition and perspective, and inculcate aesthetic disciplines – which was, after all, the precise function of its predecessor, the Academy School in the Royal Institution edifice built by Playfair on Princes Street, which became the Royal Scottish Academy. Prior to 1908 it was the nation's seat of art education; its sense of values was immutable.

By the 1920s younger members of ECA staff – several of whom had survived the 1914–1918 war – had studied in France and travelled in what was then called "the Continent," worked alongside painters like André Lhote, Amedée Ozenfant and Fernand Léger in Paris ateliers, visited London regularly and responded to paintings they saw in the commercial salons and reproduced in fine arts magazines. The 1922 Group, nine artists – including

Gillies, MacTaggart and Crozier – who had emerged from ECA's first post-war graduation that year, who thought of themselves as like-minded professional modern painters, banded together to mount annual shows. From 1923 to 1928 they made a significant, if critically unappreciated, contribution to the artistic life of the capital and even forayed to London.

The major radical influence in Scotland, however, was the Society of Scottish Artists. Back in 1891, with a missionary zeal that now seems remarkable, the newly-formed SSA set out to promote the work of its members, introduce the public to every new trend in modern art, and demonstrate the dramatic developments in Europe. Its members' annual exhibitions, in the hallowed halls of the RSA, were enhanced by distinguished foreigners. Monet, Manet and Rousseau were invited artists in 1902. Cézanne, Van Gogh, Gauguin and Matisse added a special lustre in 1913. In 1919, when Willie Gillies – just back from the war – was returning to his studies, Anne Redpath, who supported the society throughout her long career, exhibited with the SSA for the first time. By 1922 Picasso, Daumier and Degas were being hung. And in 1931 the SSA created a storm – "if this is called Modern Art, then God help us!" was a typical reaction – when no fewer than 12 major works by Edvard Munch astonished the lieges. Nothing

"Polperro"

daunted, the SSA presented Paul Klee in 1934. That same year, in another part of the gallery, you could have bought a Picasso pastel for £210 or etchings by Picasso, Matisse and Dali for £5 each.

Slowly but surely many ECA teachers of the time absorbed the metamorphoses without actually taking up arms in the revolution. On their own easels, away from their classes, painting for pleasure – and profit from the very occasional sale – many of them began to adopt a different attitude to colour, experimented with technique, overturned laws of composition and tonal values, tinkered with abstraction and symbolism. Out of this velvet rebellion emerged what would become known as the *belle-peinture* school of Edinburgh painting – inspired by Matisse, Braque, Bonnard and Vuillard – with Anne Redpath, William Gillies, William MacTaggart, John Maxwell, Henderson Blyth, and Penelope Beaton leading the way. But the teaching philosophy of the college, founded on classicism's first commandment – "thou shalt resist all change" – relented only to the extent that "there will be time for experiment after you have mastered the basics." The walls of the academic citadel had been stormed, even dented, but in no way breached.

Hubert Wellington, trained at the Slade, came from London to be principal of ECA from 1932 to 1942. Any hope that he might relax the academic ritual was soon dispelled by his erudite authority as a critic; he believed in a kind of creative demolition, pulling down in order to build up – "he'd plant a thought in the hope that it might explode into something else," Philipson remembered. Wellington was looking at a Philipson portrait one day. "Who painted this sad-looking woman?" he asked. A bit sheepish, Philipson admitted "it's mine." "Good God," said Wellington, "no wonder she's so sad." Philipson harboured no resentment of the college's rigid disciplines or of criticism which seemed at times to be personal and savage. On the whole he looked back on student life with affection, with a fondness for an ethos that stimulated him to such unrelenting industry and curiosity. He admitted that in his own long teaching career he sometimes employed Wellington's "negative encouragement" as a spur to a student's development – a gently mocking deflation, but never unkind.

Samuel John Peploe, former pupil of the Academy school on Princes Street, who had absorbed the lessons of Cézanne and Matisse, whose jazzy work had been exhibited in Paris, New York and London, who had been elected RSA in 1927 – one of whose paintings had even been bought by the French Government – had returned to his native city and taught two terms at ECA in 1933. It is still acknowledged that the place was never quite the same again.

When Philipson arrived from Dumfries in 1936 he could not have known that Dali had just painted his *Giraffe on Fire*, that Epstein had startled the world with *Ecce Homo*, and Mondrian was putting the finishing touches to *Composition in Red and Blue*. The "hick from the sticks," as he thought of himself then and for some time to come, was slow to realise that in relative terms even Edinburgh was a cultural hinterland, not much nearer the heart of things than bucolic Dumfries.

The four-year Diploma Course at Edinburgh put heavy emphasis on drawing, and as the weary student sketched for the umpteenth time yet another copy of a sculpted portrait or lifeless torso from the great Albacini Collection, he knew he was condemned to yet more drawing. Every corridor was crowded with sculpture, every cupboard and window-ledge jammed with plaster casts. Substantial parts of every day were spent sharpening pencils. For some it was the start of a lifetime habit, a daily exercise, like a pianist at the keyboard, a dancer at the barre, a singer running through scales. Philipson had a natural facility, worked hard at expanding it, acquired considerable skills, but abandoned drawing as a ritual as soon as he could. He had learned much from Edinburgh's French influences, begun a lifelong affectionate relationship with Gillies, became absorbed in – and actually excited by – the technicalities of the artist's craft, discovered secret things through the tutelage of Penelope Beaton and John Maxwell, and went off to war hopelessly in love with paint, besotted by its mysteries and magic.

TOM LOCHHEAD – Even in his early student days I was convinced that Robin would be a great painter. He studied so much. His paintings were founded on anatomical knowledge. He could be a careful painter, and he broadened out, but at the back of it all he had that sound basis of knowledge. There were one or two other students around whose painting might have been more noticeable. At the time I would have placed Robin – oh, I don't know – I'd say maybe Robin would have been about third. His work was… distinguished. He was well ahead of me, for instance. I've tried to think where I would place myself at that time. I'd come about tenth, or twelfth in the group. Robin seemed to have confidence right from the start. Something special about him. Even at school he sometimes wore a bow tie, even then, in the early 30s. And he had some mannerisms – a touch of the Prince of Wales – that went with the tie.

That caravan I was building at Dumfries… Robin and I came to Edinburgh together and stayed together. We shared digs in Marchmont. We had only an hour between classes at lunchtime and the landlady wasn't always ready for us, so we had a rush to get back on time. When we talked about living in the caravan the other students just laughed at us. The caravan was just single-skinned, but we spent the summer double-skinning and fitting it up and looking for a site within reasonable distance of the tramway. A farmer at Bonaly let us park in a field and fifteen minutes in a No 9 or 10 tram took us right to the door of the college. We stayed there all day – chips and pies in the dining room at lunchtime and then at teatime we nipped out for some rolls, brewed up tea in the metalwork room and went back to work. In the evening we had the place to ourselves. Came in at nine in the morning and left at nine at night. For three years. The fourth year, being our diploma year, Robin wanted something more settled so we moved out of the caravan back to Marchmont.

A friendship has to be strong to last three years in a caravan. We got on fine. You see, we weren't competitive really… As I said, Robin was by far the best, but he did say one time that my treading on his heels was an incentive for him too.

The high priest of classicism at ECA before the war was David Alison, RSA (1882–1955), one of Philipson's most distinguished predecessors as head of painting and drawing. A fine portrait painter – he regarded Titian as "a guid heid painter" and Raeburn as the master portraitist – Alison earned his nickname "Bouff" for his gruff, monosyllabic treatment of students.

ROBIN PHILIPSON – In my student time from 1936 to 1941 Alison would say, "Ye dinnae dae it like that, lad, ye dae it like this…" and you got it as blunt as that. Then he would do a little demonstration, a small head, beautiful. I would have liked him to paint the belly, which was giving me the most awful problems, but he didn't. These small heads of his, in beautiful vermilions and ochres and cobalt blues, he would paint them on top of the black and green torsos that I was struggling like hell with, and he would say "Oh, don't you think that's an improvement?" and I would say "I really do, Mr Alison." Then Willie Gillies [another distinguished future head of drawing and painting] would come along and say "What on earth are you going to do with that bit (pointing to the belly) now that you've got that bit (Alison's head) to contend with?" I said I didn't know, and he said "Well, I'd put a new head on it." Alison certainly imposed his style on you. Gillies never did. He told you to do what you were doing but to do it better.

JACK FIRTH – Robin had left his student training with a sound professional foundation in his craft. For four years he had drawn every day, for the last two he had painted up to eight hours for five days every week. If his sense of colour had not yet developed, he was an extremely well-disciplined and proficient painter. You know, artists of his generation went on regarding themselves as students after their formal training; one was just beginning, just removing the "L" plates. One was never allowed to forget the seniority and experience of one's mentors. Robin's natural style of painting was free and flowing, confident in the handling of paint. Paint was for him more than an essential tool – he began to need it and the need was sensual as well as intellectual.

ROBIN PHILIPSON – There was a man at the college called Charlie Howison, one of those giants thrown up every now and again for the benefit of students. Charlie ran the practical painting department, the craft of decorating, and three nights a week he went on about "fastidious adhesions" and he made damned certain that they were. He had a technique for priming canvases and we were lucky to have his advice – it was free. He mixed up paint for us in a tin, and gradually we became aware that this man was a fund of knowledge. For my part I realised that he knew everything about lead paint, zinc paint, mixing different kinds of paint. It was a revelation. I took to going there when nobody else did. He took to welcoming me. I learned a vast amount about the behaviour of white lead, how it yellows if you mix it, cleaning your boards properly, sandpapering between each coat, and then he taught me how to put gesso down on a board with a trowel. He also passed on a basic behaviour awareness – you never lost the notion of what was happening underneath what you were doing. After the war, I suddenly thought, oh lord, how do I prime my canvases, and happily Charlie was still there. We became good friends all over again and he gave me a curious A to Z – technical foundations, technical behaviour of paint – which moved into the back of your head somewhere, so that you unconsciously controlled your material and it behaved itself. Unless you wanted it to misbehave, and that was often legitimate, and worth knowing.

I remember building up my own style of painting – and it really was a mushy kind of coagulated mess – trying to get it right. Sometimes you ended up with something that was really quite attractive – these occasions were few and far between – but nevertheless they didn't single you out for the kind of arena praise they would get today. I think it's a mistake to allow young people to make drastic failures and not tell them they've made drastic failures. Most of them would walk out, but that wouldn't be any harm done, because half of them would walk back in again, or maybe more than half. Like the girl who walked out of my class in Colorado because I wouldn't enrol a sheepdog along with her. I asked her what her sheepdog was going to do with a paintbrush. And she said it wasn't a question of that, it was his presence, and the other students might want to… you might even take a brush and paint him yourself. I said I might and that might be my total undoing, so I think what we're going to do is have your dog enrol in some other discipline and you're going to enrol in this discipline. She was the bane of my life, the wee scallywag. She enrolled herself and gave me an awful time.

I think of my student days with enormous pleasure. Wellington was long gone when I returned from the war, but he'd been invited back to Edinburgh to give a talk or something to the SSA and I met him on the steps at the Mound and thanked him for some of the things he had taught me. "Parting your hair on the other side now, are you?" I was amazed that he could remember me in such detail, and said so. "No," he said, "artists should always notice such things."

I sold a painting for the first time when I was still a student. A commissioned portrait of a boy who was the fattest boy I think I'd ever seen. It was a full-frontal, as they say, with knees really like

"Mexican Altar"

cherries, massive red knees, and I painted him sitting on a little oak settle. Ultimately the father said to me, well there we are, we've come to the point of payment. Well, I remember I paid twelve pounds ten shillings for the frame so I thought, damn me, that's a lot, so I'd better charge £15 for the whole painting. I said £15 and he said that was quite ridiculous, far too much. He ended up paying only for the frame. I decided two things. One, that I was no use at business, therefore I'd remain an academic. The other one was that because this man had, in a sense, swindled me, I should stay away from portrait painting. I've stuck almost rigidly to that. Flippantly, you could say that I've never accepted a portrait commission because of that memory. But, more seriously, unless I choose the subject I go to pigs and whistles when I confront an individual. I just couldn't do it.

"Jimmy" – the Glasgow evacuee

I have a completely different attitude to another student portrait, done in my third year, back home for the summer hols. I've resurrected it; it's up there on the wall. He's Jimmy, a wee Glasgow evacuee living in our house. I painted it one afternoon in the kitchen while my mother was making toast for tea. I was down on the floor and saw him just sitting there, so I said hang on, I'll paint you. I was unusually swift. It often happens like that with a picture, and people say it must have painted itself. It probably did. I showed it to Peter Westwater and asked him what he thought. "You'll never know how good it is," he said. And I knew him well enough by that time to know that he'd coupled enormous insult with enormous compliment. Unless you knew how fastidious Peter was in his analysis, black affront would have been the most typical reaction.

CHAPTER THREE

THE OUTBREAK OF WAR IN 1939 DID NOT AFFECT COLLEGE LIFE IMME-
diately. Students in the early years of their courses were called up
as the crisis deepened, but those in their diploma year were
allowed to complete their painting and drawing course before
being conscripted. Philipson, drafted into a famous infantry regiment – the King's Own Scottish Borderers – found himself bayo-
neting imaginary Germans with a broomstick, route-marching
and square-bashing at Berwick-upon-Tweed – "cold as bloody
charity it was, sometimes, but exciting, too. I was terrified, terrified out of my wits." The "phoney war" was over, Churchill was
at the helm, the aerial Battle of Britain was being fought over the
English Channel, and Britain was still in great peril.

He enjoyed the tough life of the barracks, made friends with
rough but jolly company – gallus wee Glaswegians and daft
Irishmen he remembered with particular affection – and his natural gaiety, which responded so readily to congenial company,
was stimulated by the egalitarian fraternity of the army billet.

"What did you do in civvy street?" was an easy enough question
to answer for the miners and plumbers, joiners and lorry drivers
lumped alongside each other in adjoining bed-spaces. "I'm an
artist" was at first difficult to declare, but Philipson – who had
been indoctrinated in the belief that his Diploma of Art was no
more than a passport to a vocation – began to enjoy its unusual
distinction. When the swaddies descended on the town for
Saturday-night "jigging" his refined manners and good looks, his
spirited love of dancing – as well as that diffident artistic qualifi-
cation – greatly enhanced his chances with the local damsels.

For different reasons these same characteristics, allied to his
committed application to the sweaty process of becoming a soldier, marked him out for promotion. "He was always officer material," says Tom Lochhead, remembering how the young Robin
had been made head boy in the Dumfries Academy boarding hos-
tel. Philipson was despatched to OCTU – "the previous commanding officer had been cashiered for brutality and his successor wasn't all that much better" – and soon commissioned. After
a spell with the 9th Battalion of the KOSB at Alvaston he volun-
teered for service in India.

He served two years with the Royal Indian Army Service Corps,
travelling all over the sub-continent, but was then sent to Assam's
frontier with Burma – "we were glorified Pioneer Corps, really,
humphing trucks and ploughs and stuff all over the place; wherever it was needed we took it." Dimapur was very close to the bat-

tlefront with the Japanese for possession of Kohima and he ran the gauntlet up and down the road with vital supplies to and from Manipur. Unless he was talking about the beauties of a country he came to love, the gentle Naga tribesmen who cultivated the terraced foothills and the profusion of flowers strewn through the valleys, Robin said very little about his time at the Burma front. Tom Lochhead, himself a committed pacifist, nevertheless admired the man who had "led a rearguard action through northern Burma, an acting major, blowing up petrol supplies with the Japanese armies treading on his heels."

At that time his sister Phyllis was in Italy, doing welfare work with servicemen. Regular letters from the twins to each other survived the dismal uncertainties of wartime mail. "He wrote about the pain of seeing so much beauty destroyed – not only life, but all the wonderful things around him. He just couldn't bear it." Phyllis believes that, as a result of his experiences at the Burma front, at one point her brother became "not very well." He recalled meeting a colonel "whose war was over – I don't know what kind of soldier he was, but he was a brilliant organiser" – who had been asked to set up a big welfare camp at Singapore for survivors of the jungle war. "He winkled me into this and made me the welfare officer – I was a much better welfare officer than any other kind." He organised concerts and art classes, arranged film shows, taught leatherwork — "all the old stuff, punches and thongs" and helped battle-weary jungle fighters to design purses and handbags to send to their women back home. "These lads started their latrine duties at three in the morning so that they could be in the workshops with me at five. I worked out designs for them, helped them draw a small scene. It was, in fact, very creative."

Philipson sketched compulsively throughout his time in India and Burma but painted rarely. At Singapore he was encouraged to produce a few portraits of brother officers, with such success that his eccentric colonel offered to set up a lucrative sequence of commissions back in Blighty – "he assured me it would be as easy as falling off a wall." Still uncertain about the painting style he would eventually adopt, he had already rejected portraiture, and knew that, however much he respected them, he had no wish to become a landscape painter and take part in Bill Gillies' tented Highland safaris – "six watercolours before a breakfast fry-up" – with Bobby Henderson Blyth, John Maxwell and Willie Wilson. Already fascinated by the textural manipulation of paint he was naturally attracted to the *belle-peinture* French painting of the Edinburgh school, its colourist richness and decorative splendour, but did not want to become another Redpath or MacTaggart – or another anybody, when it came to that.

There is no doubt that he had already decided that he wanted his painting to say something, without being didactic. The problem was double-edged. Throughout his life he avoided intellectual debate by affecting a polite boredom or feigning ignorance. He concealed a belligerent intelligence behind bland diffidence. Like Sam Goldwyn he believed that "messages should be left to Western Union." He was not even sure, as a 25-year-old war veteran when he returned to Edinburgh in 1946, that anything he had to say was worth saying. Above all, and couched very much in the inquisitive tones of the post-war social revolution, he wanted his work to ask as many questions as it attempted to answer, to identify himself at the most intense level with his subject. Slowly but surely he realised that he was heading towards an emotional, expressive form of abstraction – the refraction of reality, preferring allusion to exposition, emphasising differences between poetry and prose, exploring the continent of dreams, exorcising ghosts and slaying dragons, revealing substance in shadow, playing music that only he, the artist, could hear. That was the spiritual gist of what he wanted to speak about; how he found the voice would remain for some time another, more complicated, matter.

His army experiences had shocked his sensitivities. He had seen violent death and brutality, naked aggression and mindless destruction. He knew, as all his comrades on the boat home knew, how lucky they had been in war's hellish lotteries. According to his old friend Jack Firth, "Robin regarded his army service as an enormous and frustrating gap in his painting life, but he was grateful also for the years of compressed experience it had given him." The cruelty he had seen disturbed him deeply for the rest of his life. It would appear in his work in many forms, focussed by design, heightened by the juxtaposition of colour and texture of paint. But he spent even more of his painting life blessing the luck that had borne him home unscathed and filling canvas after canvas with images that celebrated, in so many searching ways, his survival.

To put a proper end to the course he had started at ECA in 1936 he had to attend the one-year teacher-training course at Moray House College of Education. After the relative high jinks of an art college the petty schoolmam strictures of Moray House were a frustrating coda to college education at the best of times; for young men just home from the mayhem of a long war they were insufferable. Philipson recalled that year only for its scally-wag hilarity. He had Alan Davie and the Glasgow painter and critic Martin Baillie among many ex-Service accomplices – "dear me, what a ball we had!" In the first term there were many performances of a ribald pantomimic version of *Little Nell* – "Alan Davie wrote the music and the rest of us got up the words and ditties." Davie was also behind a wheeze in February, 1947 – not a leap year – when he pinned up a poster announcing that Picasso would be visiting the college on February 29. "The show we put on was a load of absolute nonsense but we had great fun doing it.

I used to play the bottom end of the piano while Alan played the top end until I could stand his noise no longer." He acknowledged that the college authorities must have had "one hell of a job" assessing their aptitude as teachers – "we spent so much time having fun they could have had nothing to go on, really, but we all got good marks."

The qualified teacher was never destined to fritter away his life as an art dominie in a Scottish secondary school. It is probably true to say that a one-term job was "found" for him at ECA – as assistant librarian, no less (and certainly no more). "I was suddenly asked if I'd like to try a very modest job with an incredibly modest salary." Charlie Howison gave him his refresher course on priming canvases. Reluctantly, he painted portraits, as technical exercises rather than anything else, and succeeded in having that modest work hung at the 1947 annual shows of the RSA and SSA. Phyllis has fond memories of a self-portrait from that period – for a long time lost but recently recovered in Edinburgh – with the young artist, bow-tied and floppy-haired, standing alongside a doll's house he had built. He was developing his free and fluid painting style, becoming bolder and more adventurous with colour, and taking advantage of many carefree hours leafing

"Gardenstown"

through the college's books where, among the giants of the past and the great European leaders of the modern movement, he found a man whose work would inspire the beginnings of his career as a painter.

Right at the start of our hours of intense conversation, with the first of many reels spinning silently on the recorder – from the beginning he was oblivious of the microphone – Robin repeated, with a squirm of impatience that seemed to surge through his frail body, his anxiety to be irritated. He failed in that ambition, if indeed he had ever seriously considered it: irritation is often irrational and a thief of time, and besides, it was not in the nature of the man to be petty. Although very ill and gravely debilitated he never allowed remembered hurts or slights, his memories of professional or social behaviour which fell below his own high standards, his having to suffer unconsidered and ignorant criticism or any other annoyance, to shroud his natural gaiety or stifle his irrepressible optimism. He might mention irksome things that were relevant, then quickly pass on with a shrug of resignation. The one dramatic exception was likely to be mere mention of Oskar Kokoschka.

It would be fair to say that he fizzed. There it is on Reel 1 in my archive: we had touched on childhood, schooldays at Dumfries, his army service, and were talking about his return to ECA after the war, how the young staff were all of-an-age, talking less then than they do nowadays but painting more, how they mounted exhibitions in the college, read a great deal, and watched the work of their colleagues "almost brushstroke by brushstroke – we

"Allegory"

learned with and from each other." I suggested that in his day they had eventually relaxed and operated a more informal *atelier* attitude. He agreed, and regretted that it seemed to have been abandoned. I applauded Glasgow School of Art for maintaining the *atelier* system and he immediately recollected somebody writing that if he, Philipson, had studied at Glasgow his "manipulative skills" would have been more thoroughly developed and he would have got "where he wanted to be" much quicker.

He didn't agree with that view, but went on to ruminate about his manipulative skills, how they were as frail in his student days as his command of language. "I had to work very hard at them and they developed very slowly." And without a pause for breath he went on: "At the end of the day, apart from being mystified by the beauty of Kokoschka's work, I didn't actually deliberately choose to follow him to the extent that has now been stressed."

There it was, out in the open from the start, *his* first mention – not mine – of the Austrian-Czech expressionist with whom Philipson is so constantly linked. As recently as 1992, in his scholarly award-winning survey, *Scottish Art: 1460–1990*, Duncan Macmillan, curator of the University of Edinburgh's Talbot Rice Gallery, found it necessary to make the Kokoschka connection in almost his first breath. That was enough to light Philipson's touch-paper – "why do they do it, it's so bloody boring" – but he went up like a rocket when, a few sentences later, Macmillan suggested that the Kokoschka inspiration "led to Philipson developing technique as an end in itself. A large view of Edinburgh Castle, *The View from my Studio Window* (1954, Hunterian), for example, is a handsome and effective tribute to Kokoschka."

That bald sideswipe about technique will have to be addressed at another time, but the soubriquet Mister Technique, often applied to him as a back-handed compliment, bedevilled Philipson – because he believed it was also used in an attempt to diminish him – almost as much as the seemingly inevitable connection with Kokoschka.

William Hardie, in his 1990 update of *Scottish Painting: 1837 to the Present*, repeats a tale that has been represented by various commentators: "Like almost all his generation, Philipson saw service with the Army... during which he fortuitously discovered and devoured a book on Oskar Kokoschka." Several writers, perpetuating the same myth as Hardie, have identified the book as Edith Hoffman's biography of Kokoschka. Philipson's version, which only he could know, is that the two books which he carried in his knapsack throughout the war were his army-issue Bible and Tolstoy's *War and Peace*. It would have been difficult for him to have included the Hoffman book, the first study of Kokoschka in English, in his wartime reading: it was not published until 1947.

"The View From My Studio Window"
(1954, Hunterian)

By that time, Philipson admitted, he was indeed fascinated by Kokoschka. He had read and re-read his essays *On the Nature of Vision* (which were reprinted in the Hoffman biography). Illustrated art books, especially the few which employed colour, were well beyond the means of most students. European art, like so much else, had been laid low, scattered and fragmented by the war. Paper rationing all but dried up new reference sources. But Philipson's incarceration in the college library, with time on his hands and a voracious hunger for visual stimulus, gave him a privileged preview of anything new that got into print as well as a refresher course in art history.

He bought Hoffman's biography and read it many times. Kokoschka was still struggling for recognition in Britain, but the

"old master, born late" and "a terrible wonder" as the poet Else Lasker-Schüler called him, was already established alongside the leaders of European expressionism. No fewer than nineteen Kokoschkas had been included in a large exhibition of what Hitler called "degenerate" German art at the New Burlington Galleries in London in 1938.

In an essay *The Development of a Painter*, which he has generously made available to me, Jack Firth documents "the Kokoschka period" of Philipson's work and how, in remembered conversations, its legacy had affected his friend:

He discussed it freely, honestly and often. Ill-considered accusations that he had aped Kokoschka, or borrowed his style, or even that he was guilty of some form of plagiarism were sometimes referred back to him and were brushed off with amusement or mild annoyance. "If it was meant spitefully, they can go hang" was a typical reaction. Critics who do not understand the process of artistic influence sometimes imagine cheating or other dishonesty. Robin talked freely about Kokoschka's effect on his work and on his approach to paint-

ing: he admired the man, was a lifetime student of his painting, and had nothing to hide. That 1938 London exhibition, which I saw as a student on a "gallery visit," might have kick-started Robin's career earlier (though somehow I doubt that), but Philipson did not see it and had to wait until after the war before seeing anything by his exemplar. It is very doubtful if, prior to 1947, the name of Kokoschka meant anything to him.

Throughout his entire career Philipson felt a genuine debt of gratitude to the master from whom he had gleaned some of the secrets of the language of paint. The echoes of Kokoschka's subject matter and even his titles – not only in Robin's early days but from time to time throughout his exhibiting career – were not a continuation of the "influence" but a conscious act of homage.

Philipson regarded the Kokoschka connection as instruction rather than influence. "Of course it was. Influence involves the acceptance or imposition of values, and that can be dangerous to a struggling person... to a person who really doesn't quite know which direction to go in. There are all those flights of steps which have to be taken – it's a most hellish process. As a teacher I always found it an awful dilemma. So I can afford occasionally to get hopping mad with the Duncan Macmillans of this world and all the people who say 'Oh, without Kokoschka he couldn't have done a blinkin' thing.' That's simply not good enough. What I tried to become had nothing to do with Kokoschka".

There was, as it happened, one Kokoschka painting in Edinburgh – a gift from the Czech Government in exile, donated to Scotland in 1942 as a gesture of solidarity and friendship. It was held in store by the National Gallery of Scotland and after the war became part of the tiny nucleus of the Scottish National Gallery of Modern Art. *Zrání [Summer]* shows a girl bathing in a stream under a bank of trees; there are other figures in a sunlit landscape; the picture symbolises the period of rest immediately following the ripening of harvest. It is a characteristic Kokoschka, painted in his early 50s, confidently complex in its fusion of underpainting and impasto, its long, fluid brushstrokes and oily glazes, its scumblings and painterly devices. Philipson became so obsessed by it that he had only to appear at the door of the NGS for the attendants to open the store, put a chair in front of the painting, and leave him to stare at it for hours on end. Jack Firth says of it: "The canvas has the vibration and pulsation of Kokoschka's personal language – his voice. A swell of gestural movement rises in paint from the foot to the top of the picture; nothing is static. This was the language Robin wished to acquire."

Philipson and Kokoschka met three times – for the first time [in either late 1947 or early 1948] after Robin made an audacious telephone call in London, and later, twice, at "dinner-jacket affairs when we acknowledged each other with not much more than a wave."

I rang him from the Tate Gallery. It was about four in the afternoon and he said, "Well, who are you, anyway?" and I said I'd just come from Edinburgh where he had a very lovely painting. "I actually find your painting enormously exciting and I would like to say hello at some point, but I'm leaving tonight to go back to Edinburgh." He said, "In that case you'd better come straight away." So I went to a flower shop and there was one lily – it cost me seven pounds, but I bought it – and I thought this is an adventure that's unlikely to be repeated. When he met me at the door he said, "You're too small for what I expected – you're not tall with a black beard, which is what I did expect... This is my wife Olga" – and turning to her – "Olga it's really just a boy who's come." Then he added, "And a very extravagant boy, indeed." And she said, "Come forward and see why." There, in a vase in a corner of their living-room, was another single lily. Olga said, "Oskar got a row this morning for buying me that."

Then he showed me this lovely series of pictures, and they were all small and so intimate, and he was almost timid about them as we sat in that small room for quite a long time. It became obvious to me that this was a very valuable historical moment in my life, but it would cost me another night in London if I didn't catch the night train. They invited me to stay the night, but a little bell rings when you know that this is only courtesy of a very special kind.

That one evening stood out like a massive landmark, a launching pad. Something was brought about by a kind of fellowship. In our conversation that night I was totally astonished at the fact that I wasn't as ignorant as I thought I was. Somehow I was inspired to place relationships and evaluations in a kind of chronology that he found quite interesting. He put it down to a Scottishness, and I found that very enlivening. I was profoundly attracted to the man's work and it made an enormous difference meeting him. How simple it all was, and innocent, and then I begin to think, golly, it wasn't simple at all. He was just a great man.

Philipson felt no need to admit or deny Kokoschka's effect on his early work. He was deeply moved by the older painter's lyricism and expressionism and held him in the same high regard as the other teachers – Alison, Gillies, Maxwell – who had made their mark on him. They had taught him grammar and vocabulary; from Kokoschka he learned how to sing, and in the process found his own voice. He had no wish to say the same things as Kokoschka, had not at that time endured any of that man's deep-rooted psychological suffering, but empathised with him – "can you imagine sitting under a damned tree with a rifle wobbling a bayonet at your chest" – and needed to know how to paint emotion, depict the "experience in life" which Kokoschka believed was the essence of expressionism. The mere replication of reality would never be enough for him: he sought to express what Otto Breicha has described in an essay on Viennese expressionism as "what lies beyond and under the surface, the essence concealed in the appearance, the beast lurking in our lives and relationships – but also the claims of suffering, the dignity and the beauty of ugliness."

If those who see Kokoschka loom so obviously in Philipson's work look closely enough they might find echoes of Munch's bleakness – a legacy handed down through ECA of that SSA exhibition in Edinburgh – something of Kirchner's liberty of colour and "nervous disequilibrium of the senses," a hint of Soutine's haunted melancholy and even of De Kooning, who had been influenced by Soutine and was being hailed as an American Picasso. "I felt like Kokoschka many, many times," Philipson conceded, "felt the stress of his spirit, but De Kooning seemed totally superficial."

❀

WILLIAM HARDIE – Philipson has explained the link between the influence of Kokoschka on his work: "I particularly recall my careful scanning of the National Gallery's painting *High Summer*...hoping that [Kokoschka's] creative strategy might be revealed to me... My satisfaction was in identifying the achievement of a rich plasticity of form within a limpid and impressionistic structure. I began to learn to construct through the grouping of small lightly placed brushstrokes of rapidly changing hue... I realised that I did indeed owe a great debt to Kokoschka. But it was not his style that I sought after. It was his ability to create resonances of colour and animation of the surfaces of the picture plane. It was the dynamism that was created in the forms themselves that appealed to me." Several cityscapes of Edinburgh, reminiscent of Kokoschka's wartime views of London, are as near the Austrian master's style as Philipson was ever to come.

JACK FIRTH – The cityscapes of Edinburgh which Robin painted in the middle 50s were most probably sparked off by the great series of high-level views of European cities which Kokoschka painted over a period of fifty years – Stockholm, Vienna, Berlin, Dresden, Prague, Paris, London.

MAURICE LINDSAY – There was in Kokoschka's achievement a fascinating simbiosis of the objective and the subjective, making demands alike on intelligence, skill and feeling, all of which characteristics the younger man possessed. But they were not yet working harmoniously in his Edinburgh street scenes, for in spite of their vigour and the immediate appeal of their energy of construction and colour, the young Philipson was using the high palette and free rhythms of Kokoschka without finding the objective correlatives. For all Philipson's daring handling, the subjective element is too strong. It is difficult to believe, when one looks at *Edinburgh, Princes Street* [Walker Art Gallery, Liverpool], that this heightened, ecstatic life ever existed in Edinburgh. This picture's success is thus as a Kokoschka-like view of the scene rather than as a Philipson view.

MARTIN BAILLIE – As there is a vestigial impressionism in all Bonnard's work so there is Kokoschka in Philipson – chromatic dissonances, the edgy, vehement attack of the brushwork, images more pigment than trompe l'oeil. Save in some early pastiche (excellent pastiche and what better way of thinking yourself into a style you want to build upon?) he did not make use of Kokoschka's somewhat vertiginous perspectives, holding more to the surface in a brilliant curtain of colour.

ROBIN PHILIPSON – Anne Redpath says somewhere, doesn't she, that the only two people of whom she's afraid are Joan Eardley and myself. And she says it in such a lovely way, you know. It's not a compliment or an offence. It's nothing. It's just a statement, as I'm likely to make about Kokoschka.

The Trap

CHAPTER FOUR

WILLIAM GILLIES WAS APPOINTED HEAD OF THE DRAWING AND Painting School at ECA in 1946, succeeding the long-serving and influential David Alison, and taking over the college at a critical time in its history. Many students were returning from war service – most of them matured beyond their years – impatient to make up for a serious dislocation of their lives, and more likely to question the college's catholic attitudes to art education. In Gillies' personal experience, history was repeating itself: he had had to pick up his own studies again in 1919 after surviving the horrors of the Flanders trenches.

A quiet, intensely private man, whose restless energy was matched only by his insatiable curiosity, it was difficult to believe that throughout the 30s he was regarded as an *enfant terrible*. The coveted post at ECA was awarded to a dedicated teacher who had made the college a substantial part of his life. But by that time he was also Scotland's most celebrated living painter, a master of the art of making the mood of a landscape part of its true record, whose still-lifes employed a personal synthesis of "simplification" which honoured Matisse, and in his manipulation of space paid homage to Braque. He may have looked and behaved like a college janitor – was, indeed, more than once mistaken for one – but his natural diffidence and humble eccentricity belied a fierce integrity and profound commitment to his life as a painter Philipson said of the man who taught him and befriended him, who appointed him to the humble teaching post which led to his becoming Gillies' successor: "I was always conscious of being in the presence of a singularly simple and straightforward man of massive intelligence." Gillies had taught the pre-war Philipson, admired him as a man and divined his painting potential, and when he appointed him as a lecturer believed he would become a very good teacher. They became lifelong intimate friends.

The library job had lasted only one term. In the SSA shows of 1946 and 1947 he had a portrait hung and in the latter year yet another portrait was selected for his first appearance in an RSA summer exhibition. For Edinburgh 1947 was a momentous year. Its Lord Provost, Sir John Falconer, declared open the first Edinburgh International Festival of Music and Drama, an event which has not only touched the entire adult lifetime of most of its present citizens, but fertilised the cultural life of Scotland in general and its capital in particular. Ignoring the omission of any official representation of the visual arts in that first Festival, the city's principal commercial gallery, Aitken Dott, established in 1842, celebrated the event with an exhibition of work by the Scottish

Colourist, S J Peploe, and gave his son Denis Peploe his first solo show. Philipson was to be associated with the gallery for most of his career.

He had with some difficulty acquired the tenancy of cottages at Torphin, south of the city at the base of the Pentland Hills.

> What a job I had getting into that property. The owner didn't trust me at all. He said he wouldn't have his place wrecked by students and I told him it was four years since I'd been a student – give me a fortnight's trial and the moment you see anything you don't like, our contract's ended. At first he snooped around a lot, and I assured him I wasn't running a brothel. I didn't want him snooping around. Off you go, I said, and he went. I found it very pleasant living up there. At weekends we sometimes had 40 people, usually at lunchtime. They brought picnics then we went for a walk on the hills. The man who ran the quarry up there, the shepherd from the farm nearby, and two very ancient people who lived next door to me all joined in. So we had a straggling mob going up the hill. In the summer, when the weather was gorgeous, it was very nice. I don't like cats, have never had any wish to paint them, but a little cat who was really the caretaker of the cottages trusted me, so I painted her.

At the college, now aged 31 and aware that important time had leaked away from him, he was teaching himself how to teach. He was still readjusting to civilian life. He had imagined that as soon as he was back in Edinburgh, back in an ambience of constructive creativity, taking part in the interchange of art and ideas, he would automatically rediscover a world that "evaporated, disappeared into a mist" the moment he had donned khaki. "The rehabilitation of that cosy pre-war norm was damned difficult to achieve. I had a lot of real loneliness." Out in the peace of the countryside he tried to find the method of self-expression he so ardently sought – how to make abstract statements in paint, the way a composer might declare himself at the start of a sonata, announce his theme, then by the challenge of call and response, point and counterpoint, harmony and discord, ask questions, provide answers, and resolve everything in a grand rondo.

In 1948 he was admitted as a professional member of the SSA. Travels in France produced relatively conventional paintings of olive groves and vineyards, houses and boats at Agde, landscapes and trees. Two paintings exhibited that year, however, *Brenda – Summer Portrait* (at the SSA) and *Brenda – Winter Portrait* (at the RSA) were the first public intimations of a personal relationship with a beautiful young woman Brenda Mark, and remain, along with *Brenda – Spring Portrait* (which won the RSA's Guthrie Award in 1951) among the most significant works of Philipson's early years.

By all accounts she had set her cap at him even before he returned to civilian life. They married in 1949. She was, according to all who knew her, a vibrant spirit, a friendly, outgoing personality, exuberant, stylish to the point of daring in her dress, and an accomplished fellow painter. Only now, in the 90s, is her work being given anything like its proper recognition.

Robin's sister believed it to be "probably the ideal marriage, devoted to each other, full of fun and hard work, with Brenda staying in the background and pushing Robin forward. He in turn did everything he could to encourage her painting."

Philipson's winter portrait of his future wife has her set against a snowy backdrop, a soft and curiously warm image, its rounded reciprocal rhythms contrasting tenderly with the harsh landscape. There may be something of Munch in it, but as yet no trace of Kokoschka. Munch almost certainly influenced his self-portrait *Walking Home Through the Night*, one of several canvases he had hung at the 1949 SSA. The painter, affecting a walking-cane, comes at us through a steeply receding street, a broody study in earthy browns and smouldering reds.

By 1950 the Philipsons had moved into the heart of the romantic medieval city. Their upper two floors of a tall tenement in the West Bow overlooked the Grassmarket which spills out from the base of the Castle Rock – an arena famous in history for public hangings and burnings, fairgrounds and demonstrations, and as a haven for the city's social derelicts. The Philipsons' floors ran away in dangerous slopes. The leaky roof was pierced with flight-holes for doves. The wainscotting hid secret caverns, Worms riddled the building's ancient beams. "It was filthy dirty," he remembered. "We scraped and scraped [at old paint and varnish], back to the original panelling, and uncovered over the fireplace the wreck of a seventeenth-century still-life of blackbirds, grapes and a peach." They were blissfully happy, perched on high, working hard and watching the world go by.

David Michie has an affectionate memory of the young artist-chappie in those Grassmarket days.

I came to know Robin in the late 40s when I became a student at ECA. Together with students straight from school there were those such as James Cumming and Alan Davie, who were resuming their studies interrupted by the war, and others such as Robert Henderson Blyth and Robin who were embarking on their first teaching appointments.

The college at that time was a rich mixture of optimism and diverse personalities. Robin had served six years in an infantry regiment, but he was by temperament a cavalry officer, a hussar, a dasher. He wouldn't have been out of place in The Charge of the Light Brigade. He brought with him more than a trace of his army service, frequently using army slang and some references to his experiences in

India. "No cholarky" was crisply said to boisterous students in a studio. He looked very young, younger than many of his students, dark hair, pale face, like a young Delacroix. Not tall, slender, he held himself erect, dressed smartly, always wore a bow tie, almost a dandy when out for a social evening, with his Edwardian turned-up trouser bottoms and cuffs on his jacket. He had a silver-topped cane which was flourished at the rascals who taunted him – presumably for his flashy appearance – when he walked through the Grassmarket. He liked the theatrical effect.

The Philipsons travelled abroad as much as possible, and if there was a hint of hedonism in it – they both enjoyed the sun on their backs and good food and wine – they were also seeking the stimulation of fresh experience, new subject matter, the constant learning process of looking at great art of the past in Florence, Venice and Assisi. Trips to Argenton, Menton and Cornwall produced drawings, oils and watercolours.

Philipson was still finding his way, working on still-lifes, the occasional landscape – he had even joined a Gillies safari to coastal Banffshire. He exhibited a portrait of Brenda's father and another self-portrait. For a man who, throughout his life protested his diffidence about portraiture, in those early years he tackled many, but always at his own instigation and from an intimate circle of subjects. One exception was the painting of Mrs James, a kenspeckle Grassmarket worthy who posed for him wearing a hat laden with artificial fruit. He was fond of that portrait and often wondered what became of it. Another portrait of the period, shown at the SSA of 1950, seems now to have a special significance. *Solita* was the Spanish wife of a college colleague. Her olive skin and raven hair set against a sombre red background created dramatic contrast, but it is an investigative study, exploring the sitter's character in the penetrating manner of Kokoschka's great early portraits.

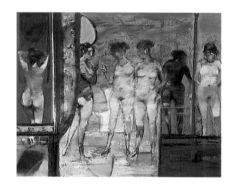

That murmur became a more positive statement in 1951 when *Brenda – Spring Portrait* won the Guthrie Award at the RSA. It is, by any standards, an important Scottish painting, a beguiling confrontation which matches detachment with intimacy, hard stare with covert glance, an embrace at arm's length. The figure is statuesque, the pose suppliant, the mood registering a mysterious votive moment in dislocated time. The vision and the engagement of emotion is Philipson's alone. There is little doubt that his intense study of Kokoschka's psychological approach – the post-Van Gogh neurotic intensity of his masterly *Portrait of Adolf Loos* for instance – helped Philipson to make his subject his emotional accomplice. And, above all, Kokoschka had taught him how to bring his own dynamic animation to the surfaces of his paint and make it speak.

❀

ALBERTO MORROCCO — I met him first with Brenda, his first wife, at an Edinburgh Festival Exhibition in the RSA. Some time in the 50s, I think. They were both bubbling over with enthusiasm (as I was) and we went around the show together making judgments as we went. He was then, as later, a snappy dresser, elegant even, and with the exotic Brenda they made a handsome couple. I remember feeling a bit of a boor in the friendly company of these two sophisticates who seemed to know all about the paintings. Robin was a little difficult to get to know intimately, perhaps because of his sometimes formal manner and cultured mode of speech, which tended on occasion to be a little high flown; it discouraged backslapping intimacy.

JOHN HOUSTON — He was obviously ambitious. He quite liked the power of decision as well as any standing he had as an artist. Brenda, I think, was a driver — and very ambitious for him. She was certainly very determined, and I think Robin was maybe pushed on a bit hard, but she encouraged him and he accepted it, then went on and kept it up for the rest of his life. She was a very strong personality.

FRANCES WALKER — He was a very stylish, even flamboyant figure, and there was always a certain theatricality about his studio appearances and presence in the college corridors. In a time of rather drab clothing — and no television — he was exotic, in velvet jacket, narrow trousers, bow tie and brocade waistcoat. I seem to recall a silver-knobbed walking stick, too. To meet this fine kenspeckle figure striding through the Grassmarket as we came down the vennel from the college was an enjoyable and entertaining experience. He seemed to us then the epitomy of an Edinburgh Old Town dandy from times past — certainly more colourful, more elegant and somewhat removed from the rest of us in the common herd. Robin remained an elegant sartorial figure throughout his life.

MARDI BARRIE — I can still picture, quite vividly, a particular jacket with subtle moss-green velvet lapels and cuffs, and of course the boundless energy and enthusiasm, and the body language, often feline. To a 17-year-old "provincial," with wavering confidence, he was a constant source of awe and wonder. There were occasions, too, when he was reassuring, with outbursts of gleeful humour, and then again, little temper tantrums, accompanied by the stamping foot!

DAVID MICHIE — He loved the opportunity to dress up — presented by the college's Christmas Revels. A favourite costume consisted of an eighteenth-century decorated frockcoat, lace collar, tall black hat with long white feathers, thin legs in black tights and large boots. He looked like a rather deranged Max Wall as governor of a remote and forgotten British Colony.

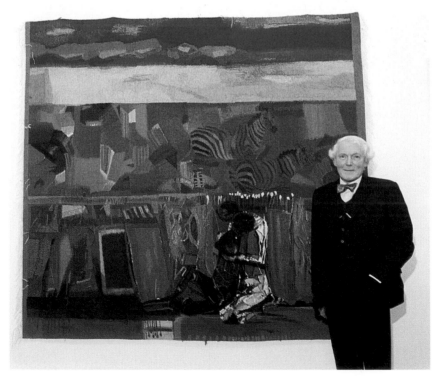

Dovecote Tapestry
"Cutting off" ceremony

CHAPTER FIVE

WHEN PHILIPSON JOINED THE STAFF AT ECA ROBERT HENDERSON BLYTH had put in his first year as a young teacher. Fraternal bonds were formed almost immediately. Philipson admired Henderson Blyth's technical knowledge and dexterity and envied his instinctive pictorial flair. Although a couple of years younger than Philipson, the new friend exuded a confidence, a cheerfully aggressive attitude to painting and criticism that won Philipson's attention and, as their relationship developed, an affection that lasted throughout their lives. Blyth by name and blithe by nature, Bobby nevertheless "tore in" with his critical analysis and, to take the Scottish vernacular even further, engaged in the tribal game of "flyting" his adversary by elevating argument into the realm of comic and poetic abuse. Robin's quick wit was a match for him, but in between fighting his corner and giving as good as he got he listened, and acknowledged that he learned from the younger man.

The years between 1951 and 1955 were filled with busy teaching weeks, even more hectic working weekends at his own easel, and foraging foreign travel throughout the long summer vacations. They cut a dash, the Philipsons, entertaining, holding inventive musical *soirées*, indulging their mutual love of decorating their home, and enjoying the cosmopolitan democracy of the West Bow – "we had Indian families below us and the smell of their curries wafted up to us through the floorboards." Philipson countered with his own olfactory nuisance. In a large bath secreted behind wood panelling he stripped old gilded picture frames in a disgusting gunge of acid and bleaches and restored them to complement the moods of his paintings.

Saturday mornings were special. A coffee-house (long gone) on Princes Street near the Mound became an unofficial club, a fountainhead of gossip and social chatter. Anne Redpath, already established as an important Edinburgh colourist, was the unchallenged queen bee of a busy hive, and the sight of Redpath and Brenda entering or leaving the establishment, occasionally draped from shoulder to ankle in voluminous cloaks, was enough to stop the tramcars.

By this time Philipson the painter was attracting some attention. The Guthrie Award had lifted his spirits and moved him up a rung or two on the local ladder. The following year he was elected an Associate of the Royal Scottish Academy (ARSA) and included in an Arts Council group exhibition *Eight Young Contemporary British Painters* in the good company of Michael Ayrton, Henderson Blyth, William Crosbie, Joan Eardley, John Minton, Julian Trevelyan and Keith Vaughan. Army life had taught him all he ever wanted to know about the joys of camping, but he again joined Gillies and Maxwell in search of subjects and a change of landscape. Cornwall offered the same escape and challenge.

Getting hung in the annual exhibitions of the RSA, SSA, and Royal Scottish Society of Painters in Watercolour was a constant aim, invariably accomplished. His titles tell us almost enough: *The Quay, Polperro; Venetian Houses; Gardenstown Harbour; Going to the Garden Party; Cornish Coastline; Perthshire Landscape.* He was invited to hold his first-ever solo exhibition in 1954 at the Scottish Gallery, following Redpath and Gillies in Aitken Dott's progressive promotion of a roster of elite Scottish painters. That year the Philipsons moved to a top flat in the New Town, a sunny home in St Vincent Street, which was large enough to give Robin and Brenda their own studios with an entrance hall spacious enough to use as a dining-room. Brenda taught art at one of Edinburgh's private schools for girls.

The most fascinating Philipson painting of this period is a large and ambitious portrait interior – Anne Redpath and her milieu, the *grande dame* herself "at home" in East London Street to over a

"Anne Redpath, Portrait Interior" (1954)

"Still-Life with Green Apples"

score of fancy folk (some identifiable, many painted from memory) lounging about or striking poses. Redpath appears in it three times and Philipson "beheads" himself at the top right edge of the canvas. *Anne Redpath, Portrait Interior (1954)* is on loan to the Scottish National Portrait Gallery. On the one hand it has the slightly satirical air of an Osbert Lancaster cartoon; on the other, its romantic expressionism, its flattened perspectives and an eruption of vermilion which overwhelms background and figures alike, give it a startling presence. Alberto Morrocco remembers Philipson telling a tale against himself in describing the reaction of a distinguished academician to the Redpath interior: "Look, laddie, what's a' that bloody red stuff a' ower yer picture? The only use for that bloody stuff is for pentin' pillar-boxes." Apart from anything else it is an interesting document, a commentary on the capital's artistic social life, its elegant *soirées* and dedication to "gracious living." It is interesting to compare Redpath's party of the 50s with another painting, from the early 80s, in the same national collection. Sandy Moffat, a student of Philipson's in the 60s, reflected the anti-bourgeois stance of Scotland's Renaissance in *Poet's Pub* – its locale a collage of Rose Street howffs, its figures a chorus of drouthy bards.

Another important work of 1954 is *View From My Studio Window* (Hunterian, Glasgow), a dramatic vista of the Old Town spine, from Castle Rock to the old tenemental "lands" tumbling down the Royal Mile towards the Palace of Holyroodhouse. The rear windows of ECA offer this spectacular view and Philipson, still in Kokoschka's thrall and challenged by thoughts of his mentor's European cityscapes, found it irresistible.

"Crowing Cock"

Philipson was still searching for oblique subject matter, images not exactly parallel to the axis of commonplace life, neither representational nor abstract, recognisable normality but slightly askew. He felt constrained by his experiments with conventional portraits and still-lifes, landscapes and interiors. Without knowing it, and certainly unable to articulate it at that time, he was looking for subjects that would generate their own energy, induce that fusion of hand and eye, the dance of brushstrokes and the interaction of colour that would create enough tension and drama to make the life of the paint itself the chief subject of his work.

Philipson admitted that, back in 1952 his friend Henderson Blyth saw what he had not seen for himself and directed him to the notebooks he brought home from Burma, and a sketch of a village cock fight in particular. "There's your picture," he said. Philipson worked up a sketch in gouache, including the fighting birds, and began to investigate how paint might create its own definition of their furious action, the slash of claw and beak, the flurry of wings and feathers. The gentle Naga tribesmen he had lived amongst and drawn at work and play amused themselves with the savage sport which was introduced to Britain by the Romans, indulged by Henry VIII and Jamie the Saxt, and made illegal in Britain in 1849.

Philipson's submissions to the RSA exhibition of 1955, the year he was elected to membership of the RSW, seemed to be ploughing a familiar field – still-lifes of decanters and fish and a pleasing double portrait of his friends David and Joyce McClure – but introduced his concept of the cock fight for the first time in public. *Fighting Cocks – Prelude*, and a study of the same subject in charcoal and wash, changed the course of his painting life.

Not content with his own sketches and vibrant, if disturbing, memories of what he had seen in Burma, he had become so fired up by the idea of cock fights as a source of creative images that he sought the unofficial and necessarily secret help of a friend, a scientist, whose poultry research department could give him access to cocks which needed no encouragement to fight each other – not to the death, as the banned sport decreed, but in deadly earnest.

The fighting went on as long as I absolutely needed it – and that was enormously helpful. I could have seen the same thing in any farmyard, but in the research lab it was controlled, contained. The drawing was fiendishly difficult. I had to find a form of shorthand. What you saw in a glance you had to hold. It's amazing, for instance, how the normal cockerel has such a long neck. They probe and probe again then move back and then you know something's going to happen. The memory of it all became so impressive and different that it became a form of creativity which pleased me and went on to please other people. Of course it all became a sequence of gestures, abstract relationships of wings to bodies, heads to necks, totally grotesque and out of character, but somehow the speed of it all, and the ferocity combined with their stateliness, their bodies joining and separating in arabesques, you knew – when it worked, when you got most of it down – you knew there was a scrap going on and a nasty one into the bargain. Of course sometimes it didn't work and you ended up with a static, absolutely chronological puffing, merely two creatures in opposition. One or two people asked me, sidled up to me as it were, wondering where I went to see the cock fights, and I said I went to a place where you can't go, and that was that.

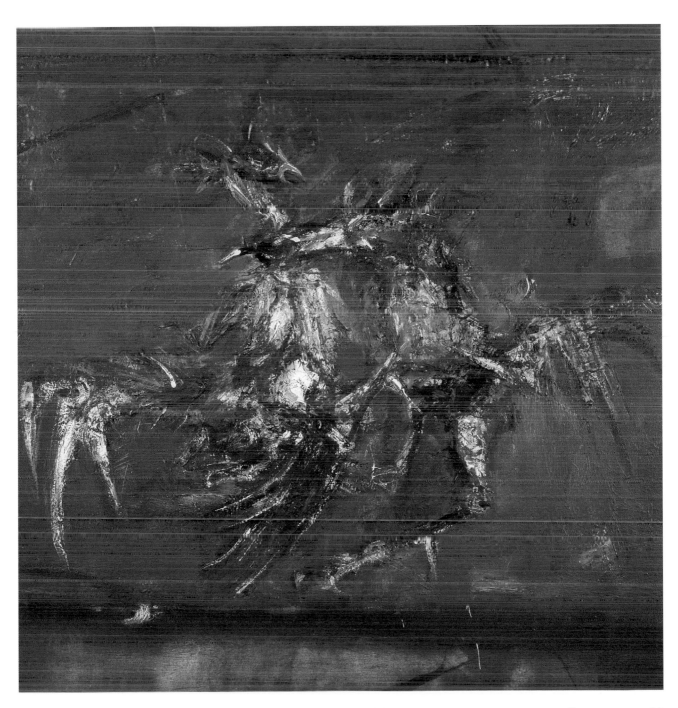

While I was painting them – and the canvases became very numerous – I suddenly realised that maybe I was going to become a thematic painter, that I didn't have to go on being one kind of still-life painter or another kind of landscape painter, or whatever. I was actually going to have to dream up and encapsulate thoughts in the form of groups of related pictures. And that's what happened at the end of the day.

The cock fights, and the immediate response to them from the public, convinced Philipson that he had found his own painting language and vocabulary. "With these pictures I moved away from Kokoschka's 'phrasing' completely." Almost everything he did owed something to classical training and discipline. Like Soutine, he had painted dead chickens, inert flesh, but had learned from the starving Jewish masochist how to make them reverberate with harmonic colour. He studied the action-painting and abstract expressionism of De Kooning, Gottlieb and Rothko – and the way Joan Eardley, in Glasgow and at Catterline, had turned the influence of these painters to her own advantage – and he, too, responded to the gestural flamboyance of New York in the 50s. Munch had advanced and retreated into Nordic gloom. Above all, Kokoschka had opened a door for him. He was able to walk free now into his own world wearing his own clothes.

❁

EDWARD GAGE – Kokoschka... at one point, became his idol. Since 1956, however, he has forged a style of his own that is entirely personal, impeccable in presentation and often stunning in its technical brilliance. But his imagery is also heavily symbolic, his themes often didactic and even grand in concept to the point of echoing the whole human predicament.

JACK FIRTH – I have looked at Robin's Burmese sketchbooks – the artist watching the villagers watching their birds fighting. He was fascinated by the spectacle, but it is also true that he was caught up in the excitement of the ritual and was not detached from its violence and blood. He drew detailed and very expressive studies of the birds and their movement the tentative prelude and getting within range to strike, the circling and display, then the stabbing, jabbing flurries of the dance of death. He was held by the whole gory horror. The theme stayed with him throughout his life. He used it as a metaphor for conflict and strife. It could pop up in the predella of an altarpiece and in his last years appear unexpectedly out of context among the hedonist delights of his *Secret Garden* paintings or alongside his *Women Observed*.

WILLIAM HARDIE – The Scottish Arts Council's *Fighting Cocks* of 1952, one of the earliest examples, remains close enough to its subject to be instantly identifiable; in later versions, e.g. *Fighting Cocks, Grey* (c. 1961: SNGMA) the paint itself, with its "strange unpredictable behaviour," all but completely usurps the place of the motif, providing an analogue for the aggression, violence, movement and energy of a cock fight while retaining an often exotic richness of descriptive colour.

LILIAN BROWSE – Colour is Philipson's most essential means of expression, the use of which characterises his basic attitude; a search for greater freedom and intensity. It is not an interplay of defined areas but an iridescent colour which avoids statements of plain juxtaposition. It may develop into explosions in which the *Fighting Cocks* are the centre of this expanding energy, remorseless and cruel.

MAURICE LINDSAY – The earliest paintings in the cock fighting series were predominantly red. Philipson then began to realise that this redness had something to do with the climate of reaction on the part of the observer – blood, "seeing red" anger, and, as psychologists tell us, the male sexual symbolism of the colour. Later he varied the thickly built-up textures with flicks of grey, white, or blue; or, in the most recent examples, yellow. The effect is the heightened quality of disturbance, which goes far beyond the merely decorative or anecdotal.

ROBIN PHILIPSON – I think the cock fight series, in my humble opinion, should be played down. The paintings aren't about what people say they're about. At the time I felt I wanted to paint designed aggression. The psychological content is very modest. I wanted them to be decorative, not tooth and claw all the time. We've had poems written about the subject, and there are old lithographs and drawings, which are very much better than the kind of things I did.

F W FENTON – As they become more aggressive, the maddened birds become also more tattered and weary. In one oil they are little more than skeletal near-white forms, and in another ragged, black, nearly exhausted birds. In *Cock Fight, Study* of 1966, two birds face each other over a panel of a colour so gentle it presages the rosewindow pictures.

"Cathedral Interior – Remembrance"

CHAPTER SIX

OVER THE YEARS THERE WERE HUNDREDS OF COCK FIGHTS SOLD TO A public whose taste seemed, at the time, contradictory. Fruit, flowers, familiar landscapes and the ubiquitous Scottish harbours and fishing boats were the sort of subjects then – and, to a high degree, still – most likely to be given pride of place above bourgeois fireplaces. Without prostituting themselves professional painters fed that gallery market. In the 50s Gillies and Redpath, Philipson and Eardley were selling small oils for less than £50 and major paintings for under £150. Into that cosy convention of still-life and flower tableaux, Highland corries and glens, Philipson suddenly introduced the grisly spectacle of birds stabbing and clawing each other to death. In hindsight public taste might now be seen to have been discriminating. If, after all, the artist maintained – as he did, even in the last weeks of his life – that the main purpose of the cock fights was decorative, people who bought them in the 50s and 60s would be justified in claiming that they had been clever enough to discern that for themselves.

Philipson was always uneasy about critical attempts to psycho-analyse his paintings. He scorned jargon and the convoluted codes of academic analysis, the posturing gobbledygook of edicts from ivory towers. As an image-maker he valued the immediate impact of his work on innocent eyes. More than once he left me with the fanciful impression that, in an ideal world, he would have preferred his work to be unveiled, curtains swished aside in his presence, and the viewer's reaction observed – not out of vanity or the need for a round of applause, but to measure the dramatic effect of a new composition, to see where the gaze lingered, to hear the comment it stimulated. A man of deep and hungry intelligence, he was no intellectual. He did not believe in the doctrine that all knowledge derived from pure reason, and would argue that artistic knowledge, the sense of a profound and mysterious wonder, sprang from other sources in the human psyche. The impenetrable thickets of art history and arid judgments from academia offended him in their attempts to put into words that which he knew he could say only with paint.

There is, of course, much more to the cock fights than mere decoration, but he would have been the last person on earth to draw attention to their gestural violence, their disturbing symbolism, the atavistic ritual of mortal combat and the pitch of unhealthy excitement to which civilised man can be stimulated by such encounters. Jack Firth observed them develop. "More and more the subject retreated and the painting took over. They started to involve light as the physical element in the picture, an el-

ement in which the birds seem to become enveloped, almost as if they were in water. Sometimes the heat of battle was whiteness rather than redness, and all the time the paintings were developing beyond the ostensible subject and becoming works of improvisation."

No sooner had Philipson decided to be a painter of themes than he began to paint, concurrently, themes in series. His 1956 *View of Princes Street* (Walker Art Gallery, Liverpool), derived from studies he had made from the top of the memorial tower on Calton Hill which replicates Nelson's telescope, was his last major work influenced by Kokoschka. It is a celebration of a city he had begun to love as his own, of one of the most startling streets in the world, and if he saw it in a high romantic light from perhaps its most dramatic viewpoint – as if the staid capital was in a state of perpetual Hogmanay – no one who loves the place will quibble. Among his exhibits at the RSW that year was a watercolour *Jousting Knights*. Philipson the boy, with one foot in England and the other in Scotland, had grown up with folk chronicles of martial chivalry in his ears, tales of endless feuds between Percys and Douglases – of armoured knights tilting at each other on caparisoned horses with ladies' favours fluttering from their lances – and spine-chilling accounts of marauding Border reivers. Chivalry and nobility and audacious derring-do were essential elements in his affection for romantic mythology, the thrill of mounted combat, its saints and villains. It was almost certainly one of the reasons why, all his life, he was so fond of Western movies.

The year after he exhibited *Jousting Knights* he visited Paris to select work from contemporary European artists for an RSA loan exhibition. It was an exciting trip, during which he met the Spanish painter and theatrical set designer Antoni Clavé, a sumptuous decorator who brought some of the gilded splendour of Spanish court scenes and church interiors to a pastiche of medievalism. Back home, and perhaps stimulated by Clavé's historical references, Philipson began to introduce the image of a king into his paintings. The mythical and often mysterious figure might be on horseback or holding court in vast interiors. These beguiling personages, like *Prisoner King* at the RSA in 1958, and *Equestrian King* which was used as the Edinburgh Festival poster of 1959, never developed into a theme – Jack Firth says Philipson ultimately forsook the kings and knights as being too superficial and seductive, "a decorative cul-de-sac" – but as potent images they patrolled his imagination and returned to haunt his canvases from time to time. *King and Hunchback*, a large canvas, brought him his first national recognition in 1959 when it won joint third prize (with Ceri Richards) as an invited artist at the second John Moores Exhibition in Liverpool. The painting stayed in Liverpool, bought by the Walker Art Gallery. Its pictorial presence is darkly majestic. Two figures in a vaulted cathedral-like limbo are

engrossed in some sinister business. The painting's ambiguity – is the hunchback Quasimodo or is he a refugee from *Las Meninas* by Velasquez? – remains impenetrable.

One dull winter day in the late 50s I visited the stained-glass artist Sadie McLellan in her studio-workshop off Byres Road in Glasgow. A huge welded steel armature stood against the daylight from two large windows. Into this frame she was setting thick chunks of chiselled glass, using the French *dalle de verre* technique. Each colour would be sculpted into the design with cement fondue. McLellan was making a new rose window for Pluscarden Abbey, the 15th-century Benedictine monastery near Elgin on the Moray Firth, to replace a window destroyed during the Reformation. The studio was covered in dust and the floor and every work surface was littered with the fragments of glass which had flown from her chisel. Suddenly the dark clouds parted, a single shaft of blazing sunshine hit the armature like a searchlight. The glass in it seemed to burst into flames and, like a lens, scatter light round the room so that the floor and the benches caught fire, until we were standing in what seemed to be an Alladin's cave of a million scattered gems. Whenever I see Philipson's rose windows, especially his watercolours where the luminosity of the white paper glows through and enriches his most vibrant colours, I am reminded of that moment in Glasgow.

He began to paint rose windows in tandem with kings and princes in the late 50s. Sometimes the subjects intertwined and cathedral interiors became common settings. He visited Amiens and, inspired perhaps by Monet, painted its exterior, but it was the lure of soaring stone arches, dense shadows pierced by lancets and circles of coloured light, the glint of ancient gold alive with candles, that sucked him inside. He was to exploit the theatricality of these Gothic interiors in many ways throughout his career, but the challenge of the rose window – its circle floated like another moon in the dark void of the universe yet contained by the rectangle of his canvas, its radiant colours set like jewels in black filigree, its medieval association with religious adoration and sanctuary – became an insistent new theme. They would be seen as serenity against the fury of the cock fights. Some would hear from them a shout of exaltation. Others would respond enthusiastically to a decorative device which ingeniously explored the refraction of light and colour, the disposition of volume and space. I asked him if it was eccentric of me to see some of the frenetic energy of the cock fights abstracted in the windows: "Not at all. You would. The windows were much more difficult to paint than the big cathedral interiors, which began to be static and architectural, so I beamed in on the windows, made them jump, switched perspectives and made the circle advance and recede. The windows took me as close to abstraction as I ever wanted to go. I had many a long think, even arguments with myself about it, and consciously decided that was far enough."

Too much has been made of his "pretty" windows. It was never his intention to spill their colours like a casket of jewels. He began by observing and admiring the grand designs that set their fine

"Rose Window and Fallen Warrior"

tracery, like frail embroidered doilies, in the severity of vaulted gothic arches and marching stone columns. When he began to divide his rose window canvases with bright stripes of primary colour – these "ladders" of paint were employed over many decades – he was trying to reinforce the structural power of the architect's design.

At the start of the decade which became the "swinging sixties" for some and a troublesome time for others, Philipson's future seemed poised on the edge of great good fortune. His second solo show at the Scottish Gallery in 1958 had won him fresh admirers in lowland Scotland, and in 1960 he was preparing for his first London exhibition at the prestigious Roland, Browse and Delbanco Gallery. Not that his first experiences there had been altogether encouraging. After helpful introductions and a formal invitation to visit the gallery he turned up, as arranged, and identified himself at the door. "Who's that down there?" bellowed a voice from an upper floor. "It's Robin Philipson." The voice, which turned out to be "the ferocious" Lilian Browse, roared back: "Get rid of him, we've got work to do." They became great friends.

That year also saw the elevation of Gillies to principal of ECA and Philipson, who had been taught in turn by Alison and Gillies, was appointed their successor as head of painting and drawing. He was 43, ARSA, RSW, and had begun to feel that he had made up for the lost wartime years. As a teacher he survived a difficult early period when he seemed a bit "too much of the officer" and not enough of "the gentleman" to many of his students and even staff colleagues. Army man management, which he had learned in the harsh realities of battle, raised the hackles of mature men and women and youngsters alike. The martinet perfectionist mellowed, and by persuasive charm, encouragement and humour succeeded where hectoring had failed. There were occasional, incandescent rows – some, to his lasting regret, never resolved – but the majority were patched up after smouldering intervals.

The idea of picking up a piece of charcoal or brush and altering student work had become anathema.

> Today's student would walk out, probably wrapping the board round your neck on the way. Then again, tutors wouldn't do it because they said it would be influencing the work. I'd say, all right, but in what way are you earning your salary? What's your tongue doing? How are you going to help these young people? I said that even doing a bad drawing for them was worth a thousand quid. Don't be ashamed. Scribble a few fast lines for them, delineate form, move on and leave them bemused. Come back in half an hour and as often as not they'll have found the answer for themselves. If you've missed it, and they've missed it, what the hell, it's been missed, it's gone, start again.

The London show was a commercial and social success. More importantly, it was noticed, and to the end of his days Philipson acknowledged the good luck that brought Eric Newton, then art critic of *The Sunday Times* to see it, enjoy it, and say so – with particular fervour in the BBC's radio discussion programme *The Critics*.

> ERIC NEWTON: We're concerned with Robin Philipson as a painter. First question: Is he a good painter? Second question: If so, what kind of a good painter?

> I think he is quite exceptionally gifted as a *painter*, which is not quite the same as saying he is a good artist. But I would not have asked you to discuss him if I had not considered him a good *artist* as well. The distinction is fairly obvious. But my point is that he is the kind of good artist who would be helpless if he were not something of a magician in the handling of paint.

> Can we define him? He has obsessions. Two of them are quite evident in the show. One is Gothic cathedrals; the strength, the complexity of their outsides, the glow and the mystery of their interiors. The other is cocks fighting; the vicious anger of their beaks and talons; the jab and the flutter and the fuss of their feathers. Anyone who can paint both these subjects and capture their overtones – the solemnity of the cathedral, the hysterics of the cock fight – is a real artist. But in order to capture overtones, he has to be an exceptional painter, a man who handles the stuff as easily and as confidently as we hope to handle words.

> ERIC KEOWN: I like him because although he's a modern painter, he does give you straightaway his terms of reference… I find him exciting for his clean, beautiful colours, both in oil and in watercolour, and for the irresistible energy he can get into a canvas. I can't remember any canvas which is as explosive as *Cocks Fighting* – two cocks tearing each other to pieces so powerfully and so rapidly that… you think the whole thing is going to explode in your face.

With that kind of praise ringing in his ears Philipson could afford to smile at the memory of a conversation with Gustave Delbanco while the exhibition was being hung. "We're going to allow your pictures the privilege of selling themselves," said Delbanco. "We're going to make no effort whatsoever on your behalf. And if your pictures don't sell I think you would agree there's no point in us doing any business together." Philipson agreed: "That's bang on, absolutely bang on. It puts me exactly where I want to be, knowing what the score is." He told me: "That was the flaw on which the relationship fluctuated and became a powerful friendship."

But 1960, a year of such success and burgeoning hope, dealt Philipson a blow that profoundly affected him as a painter and as a man. Brenda Mark, his beloved wife, the gifted painter who had sublimated her own talent to support him with such devotion and encouragement, died of a brain tumour. When it was first diagnosed, two years earlier, she survived an operation to remove it and seemed on the mend. They were living under the threat of a

relapse when her condition deteriorated and she succumbed before another operation could be attempted.

WILLIAM BAILLIE, President of the Royal Scottish Academy – I joined the staff at ECA just when Gillies became principal and Robin was made head of department. We had holidays together. The first was in Majorca, just after Brenda died. He was very depressed and needed a break. We went to see Robert Graves; we loved his poetry, but when we went to call on him he had just left for Oxford and we missed him. Majorca was at its best. There weren't many tourists in 1961. On the way back to our hotel one night a thunderstorm was brewing and it started to rain. Robin said we'd better run for it. I rather fancied myself as a sprinter, but hard as I ran I couldn't get rid of him. Suddenly we had a competitive race for three quarters of a mile and belted along with the rain pelting down and reached the hotel absolutely breathless, but almost neck and neck. I looked at him with some surprise and he said, "Aye, that wasn't too bad for an old chap was it, Billy Baillie?" He could run, all right, full of energy.

DAVID EVANS – In the way that some people in the 60s came to anticipate every new Beatles release, I remember waiting with the same anticipation to see what Robin's new pictures at the RSA would be like. He was an innovative craftsman with paint and liked his students to acquire technical skills ensuring they could develop their own personal ideas. He seemed to need to paint themes – the great cathedral pictures and crucifixions. There are many imitations, usually poor, which speak volumes for the quality of his pictures. We used to talk about technique. He told me how he used to wait ages to be able to glaze over impasto to get his lovely dark luminous passages in large oils. He was rather worried when I told him to try glazing with a mixture of turpentine and polyurethane varnish. I don't think he ever tried that!

JAMES MORRISON – I well remember the first major painting in the RSA that I saw – a Kokoschka-esque painting of Edinburgh. By that single work he seemed to reconstruct the strong ties which had existed between Scottish Art and the continent, between 1880–1920. That picture was prophetic, as his career showed him constantly influenced by a succession of European and American styles. Yet these styles were absorbed and recreated in an iconography and language which were entirely his own. What I *always* enjoyed in his work was a great sensitivity to surface. He was one of the first established figures in Scottish painting to use acrylic paint and he took full advantage of its strong three-dimensional and textural qualities.

DUNCAN MACMILLAN – The *Fighting Cock* series… did much to establish his reputation, maintain his expressive quality, but it soon began to be tempered by elegance of execution in the manner of painters like Georges Mathieu. Uppermost in his pictures, in marked contrast to Eardley's throw-away attitude, is what

Philipson himself calls "the craft of painting." He used his technical virtuosity to develop a kind of painting that was as autonomous as music without actually being abstract.

EDWARD GAGE – Though his technical virtuosity could make the banal appear fascinating, theme is of prime importance to Philipson, and its faithful interpretation, its precise translation, governs his every move. In character, his choices of theme frequently favour those with an emotional flashpoint of some kind.

DAVID MICHIE – His painting represented an interest rather different to the main influences prevailing at that time. Much contemporary painting had largely static forms and had obviously structured organisation. Robin's work, in distinct contrast, had free-flowing movement, even tempestuous forms and equally tempestuous handling of paint.

"The Covering Sea"

CHAPTER SEVEN

EVEN ALTHOUGH BRENDA MARK'S DEATH WAS EXPECTED – "IN A SENSE," recalls Jack Firth, "Robin's suffering had already taken place" – the shock when it came was profound. "He was only half-aware of his daily tasks at ECA and his good friend Gillies 'carried' him over a difficult period." Up to that time in his life Philipson had known the death of only one intimate, his 18-year-old brother John, who had drowned through what was believed to have been negligence during an army survival training exercise. In the stramash of war, isolated abroad as he was, his sorrow at that tragedy was compounded with outrage. John, his family believed, might have also gone on to become a talented painter.

Those who knew him well and could observe his behaviour found that Philipson's grief projected him into a state of numbed detachment. It was some time before he sought solace in work. "In that year," Firth remembers, "when he began to paint again, he explored a new image – the medieval ritual of burning at the stake, a symbol for human sacrifice, the taking away of life. The idea could be seen, in a sense, as an extension of his preoccupation with cathedrals and rose windows, but I believe the real motivation was the loss of a young wife whose achievement and great promise complemented his own in a marriage of mutual admiration and happiness." When I asked Robin, more than 30 years later, about the symbolism of these paintings – he was reluctant, always, to explain or even suggest what you should see in his work – he affected not to understand the question and answered with an account of the techniques he had used to achieve effects in watercolour on such a majestic scale.

The Burning, three large panels which had been painted as separate entities, came to life as a sequence of images only when Philipson spread them out on the floor of his college studio and, for the first time, saw their intricate relationship to each other. They appear to be a planned progression – from conflagration, to glowing embers, to smouldering ashes. A figure at a stake is central in all three. The fiery left panel is slashed by three dark cruciform horizontals. The central panel sets the blackened figure against a jaundiced grey and lilac around somnolent reds. The right panel is bathed in the frosty glow from a blue rose window – his planetary wheel of eternity – with the figure lifeless and charred. There is very little pictorial definition. The human form advances and recedes as if wreathed in swirling smoke and flame, so that it is never entirely fact or fancy, like the ebb and flow of pictures that one might indeed see in a fire.

Firth, an authority on watercolour technique, considers *The Burning* to be a Philipson masterpiece and, in its day, a unique triumph of technical skill allied to profundity of meaning. "The floating of the veils of colour with the trailing wisps of chalk and the complexity of the paint structure all go to make this one of the major paintings of its time, without gimmicks or tricks, but with a total control of materials and emotion." Firth acknowledges the difficulties of painting watercolour on that scale, the problems of keeping the paper wet, avoiding warping, making large quantities of pigment available to the brush, achieving such delicacies with such large brushes. "Watercolour," Philipson admitted, "holds a special fascination and magic for me – how it shapes and influences forms. During the working process many things happen beyond the level of premeditation. When a certain luminosity appears, this conditions the mood and the finality of the painting. The suspension of colour in water and the uninterrupted flow of the water all combine towards this new interpretation."

Philipson did not exhibit *The Burning* until the RSW of 1963, but in the interval returned to the subject more than once in symbolic sacrifices on wasteland and deserted shores. *Burning at the Sea's Edge*, a powerful small oil, is – like the watercolour trilogy – in the SNGMA collection.

The critic and academic T. Elder Dickson, who was seldom provoked to superlatives, writing in *The Studio* in 1963, greeted the new work with unbounded enthusiasm.

> Why so large? The question admits of no simple answer: predilection and motivation are not easily disentangled. The large watercolours... at all events, silence the captious critic and any lingering doubts we might entertain are blown sky-high by Robin Philipson's heroic trilogy *The Burning*, measuring approximately five feet by eight feet long. It would be merely silly to ask, as we may be tempted to do, "Could this not be said in a picture half or quarter this size?" We simply do not know. It was not in any case conceived in terms of the traditional watercolour nor for any specific purpose. It is a massive epic painting wrung from the artist from excess of feeling and depth of insight. For sheer virtuosity it is, as far as I know, without parallel. It has given watercolour a new dimension – dramatic – stunning.

At about this time, in one of his few public utterances about his work, Philipson was saying: "I believe that the essential meaning of my painting is made possible by the eye being carried back again and again to each area of the picture plane, but always in a different way; meaning thus makes its own unfolding through a series of intuitive acts."

It is worth noting that Philipson presented *The Burning* as three separate images, without mounts, in thin silver frames. When

Douglas Hall, the SNGMA's first Keeper, bought the paintings for Scotland's growing collection he had them united, as a triptych, in a single black wooden frame. Philipson knew nothing of the change until he saw *The Burning* in the gallery several years later. He made no formal complaint but never hid his displeasure that his presentation of the paintings had been so radically altered without consultation. Douglas Hall defends his decision to get rid of "highly contrived Aitken Dott-like frames" and present *The Burning* "as far as possible as pure naked painting." He found Philipson's attitude difficult to understand. "It indicates to me that Robin set boundaries to his work in the metaphoric as well as the literal sense, and I wonder at the necessity for this. It seems out of keeping with his early admiration for expressionism, although I suppose that in his career as a painter and a social being he followed a somewhat similar trajectory to his particular idol, Kokoschka."

By sheer will, and that compulsive need to paint which was the engine of his entire life, Philipson blazed a path through the 60s. He had got married again in 1961, to Thora Clyne, one of his students, a lass from Caithness who also had serious ambitions as a painter. "Thora's natural kindness and gentleness had helped Robin immensely after Brenda's death," his sister Phyllis remembers. "In their life together she continued to support him, a good wife who saw him through many troubled times, and had great influence on his painting career. No one could have admired his work more or encouraged him more selflessly." He had successful solo shows in London and Edinburgh and in 1962 was elected a Royal Scottish Academician. Colin Thomson, a former director of the National Galleries of Scotland who curated Philipson's massive Edinburgh Festival retrospective in 1989, said: "These were the beginnings of his public career. Scotland adopted Robin, as Robin had adopted Edinburgh." Like the circus performer keeping dozens of plates spinning on rods by dashing to each one in turn and giving it a twirl, the sequences of cock fights and cathedrals, kings and rose windows continued; he had already adopted the practice of keeping many canvases, five or six or more – "sometimes 20 on the go," as he put it – at the same time.

Despite the burden of an increasing number of public commitments, bouts of ill-health, and his conscientious administration of a college which, like all other educational establishments was having to thole change and disturbance, this "weekend painter" as he ironically described himself maintained an amazing output. There were more burnings, some fighting bulls, still-lifes, figure studies which were the precursors of harems of odalisques, but even in his most decorative mode there were often dark strands of threnody – in his precise definition "an ode or lamentation for the dead" – which, almost as if they were a reminder of a great sadness, became thematic in themselves.

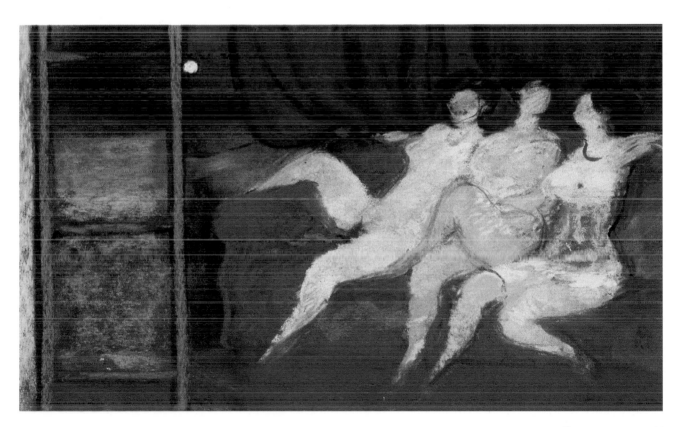

He enjoyed what he felt in himself as an affinity with poetry – a sensual response rather than literary appraisal or discrimination. From childhood he realised that he suffered from some unspecified but very mild form of dyslexia, and although he learned to use words with style and panache – there were few more engaging public speakers – reading and writing caused him problems, especially if extended over any concentrated length of time. He was by no means alone among artists in finding it difficult to give his paintings titles. In his case, when he had gone to great lengths to conceal the obvious, to avoid representation of reality, it was essential that a title should be allusive, should do no more than nudge the viewer towards a sympathetic awareness of his intentions. He was grateful to more than one friendly poet – George Bruce among them – for finding the elusive words for him.

Colin Thomson thinks the poetic analogy was also appropriate in Philipson's "quest for the rhythms and cadences that celebrate life, that express the obscure need we feel for a sense of order. A common feature of Robin's work from 1960 onwards was a sub-divided composition or, what is nearly the same thing, the tripartite form of the triptych, which he used in a number of his major works." Thomson saw poetry in these visual experiments and quoted the artist speaking about "opening up horizontal or vertical corridors in which different but related pictorial activities can take place within a single picture space." And Philipson betrayed a true sense of the sensual power of poetry when he added that a

picture's title needed to act "by its sound as much as by its sense" – a variation, had he known it, of the best advice to an actor on the brink of delivering Shakespeare – "take care of the sense and the sound will take care of itself."

In what is possibly the most spectacular studio in Britain, the coveted prerogative of the head of ECA's painting school, Philipson found room to expand. This huge working space, its north wall a vast window giving out on to Edinburgh Castle, had never known so much activity on such a scale. He could keep three or four conventional easels engaged, manipulate staging and steps to take him to even larger works suspended from the walls, even retire to a tiny room up near the ceiling for a bird's-eye view of work in progress. At a time when the bulk of Scottish painting was still being scaled to suit bungalow walls Philipson became more expansive in his ideas and in the size of canvases he used to express them. Much of his most important work could not have been accommodated in any domestic setting and depended for a home, therefore, on commercial buildings and public institutions.

Always an innovator, he constantly experimented with materials. The artist, he believed, had to be craftsman as well, needed to know all he could learn about the behaviour of paint, how to orchestrate effects, create texture, glaze, build collage, when it was imperative to observe the rules, how to boldly defy them in the spirit of adventure. Only through complete confidence in his craftsmanship could an artist give his deeply considered intentions the illusion of immediacy, the vitality of generous and impulsive gestures. He bitterly resented the pejorative implications of opinion which applauded the technical proficiency of his work at the expense of its artistic ambitions. He learned the craft of painting as a means to an artistic end from Cennino Cennini at one stage of the historic process and Charlie Howison at the other. The Renaissance master technician taught him all he needed to know about gesso and gilding; the Edinburgh housepainter showed him how to prepare his canvases; neither knew anything at all about plastic paints and acrylics and copolymers. By the middle of his career the Scottish paint manufacturers Craig & Rose were mixing colour for him to his own precise specifications – Philipson Blue, for instance – and helping him to develop the use of vinyl toluene, a substitute for the balsam of the tolu tree, as an alternative painting medium when he wanted to create special effects.

In 1963 Philipson was invited to the United States as visiting professor of painting at the University of Colorado at Boulder in the foothills of the Rocky Mountains. He enjoyed the experience, learned many things from the raw sweep of the landscape, the infectious enthusiasm of a college life much less stuffy than anything he had known, and found himself drawn to the symbolic imagery and decorative fables of the indigenous Indian culture.

A short visit to New Mexico made indelible impressions. He admitted that the visual splendour of European cathedral interiors had made his mind reel – "as if the vino had gone straight to my head" – but of course great painters of the past had taught him what to expect. "What excited me most about them was their space, something you can't really convey in representational painting. In Venice, at San Marco above all, that vast space is so beautifully lit, roundels and lancets and slits and sudden shafts of daylight, and seemingly endless shadows. I had this great desire to recreate all the visual aspects of these interiors simultaneously, blending the inspired and intricate rhythms of all these shapes and the richly saturated colour." Sheer scale caused him some anxiety. "You felt the canvas had to be so big that it might look vacuous. But I found that careful laying on of glazes, over paint thick enough to hold them, produced a very rich luminosity. It was almost as if they made a sound, a singing sound, they were so effective."

This glazing process was developed to its limits after he visited the villages of Chimayo and Sanctuario near the US border. He found the door of the church at Sanctuario, a small building made of wood and plaited grasses, locked against him. "I looked through the keyhole, through a gap in the grass wall. Bits of cloth and books here and there, crutches and other proof of miraculous cures lying about, and I could see the altar. It had no gold, only yellow paint and some simple primitive drawing, but I have to tell you it was majestic, absolutely magnificent." He looked at other Mexican church interiors, many of them lavishly decorated, "but I never again found anything to match the simple but sumptuous vitality of Sanctuario, and I wondered a great deal why this was so, and how I could express it." After many experiments he evolved a chromatic harmony of blue, yellow and scarlet. "Somehow, it defied analysis. No matter how you arranged it, moved it about, changed the relationships, the harmony survived. I struggled with it in many ways, and tried to elevate it into much bigger scenes – some of which, I have to admit, have been dismissed as failures."

DOUGLAS HALL (1970) – When one finds a sophisticated and aware artist pursuing a different direction from most of his peers one looks for the reason. Most often, perhaps, it is found in humanist convictions, as in Kokoschka himself, for whom "man is the measure of all things" and non-objective art the worst of our spiritual enemies. With Philipson, the reason appears to be a more strictly professional one, in that he seems to be compelled to pour out his professional skill with increasing lavishness. This at a time when the whole tendency of art for ten years past has been reductive, to make larger and larger statements of more and

more elementary relationships of colour and form. Philipson's latest work, too recent even to be shown in this exhibition [Carnegie Festival retrospective, Dunfermline 1970], shows almost a passion to fly in the face of the craze for simplification. Philipson is a strong painter. Yet the influence of contemporary thought in art is also strong, and all-pervading. A retrospective exhibition of a painter in full career is bound to project a question into the future, and the answer concerns the resolution of this conflict, if conflict it is.

WILLIAM BAILLIE — I always hesitated to interrupt his work. "Come on in, pleased to see you," and I'd open the door and he's covered in paint and surrounded by all these works in progress. There's one on the easel, and I say, "my God, that's coming on well, Robin." I was always amazed at how prolific he was. And he would say, "not coming too well, just a bit stuck with it, don't know what the hell to do, I think I'll just turn it upside down." I understood that, of course, it's a way of seeing how the colours are working from a different viewpoint. He would get very cross with himself when things didn't work out – probably more often than people imagine. But he was also very tenacious and believed that unless you did something, you'd still be cross with it the next morning. I never saw Robin as a facile painter. The work didn't trickle off the end of his brush in the manner that some people would have us believe. He worked damned hard at his craft to make the kind of images and get the luminosity he desired.

ROGER BILLCLIFFE – Philipson is an obsessive painter. He is never relaxed unless he is in front of a canvas with a brush in his hand and even then the nervous energy which drives him is just as apparent. It was this energy, this painting, with technique, with discoveries yet to be made, which accounts for the prodigious amount of work which he produced in the 1960s and 1970s.

LILIAN BROWSE – Although Robin experimented with various media in order to achieve certain effects, the pictures in oil paint were predominant. Whether handling it in free, apparently random brushstrokes or in thick impasto, his delight in the medium is evident, but he never allowed his enjoyment to run away with him, for a self-discipline was inherent… His subjects are based on buried experiences, whether joyful – rose windows and cathedral interiors with their beautifully lit spaces – or compassionate, as instanced in the horrors of war.

JACK KNOX – In his painting he was a superb craftsman in complete command of his language, yet constantly probing and questioning his art, and I had the feeling that by the time his experiments and discoveries had begun to suggest to him foreseen conclusions, he was already turning his attention elsewhere. While the directions taken by the new work were always surprising, looking back over the great series he embarked upon, from the cityscapes of Edinburgh, the group portraits of friends, the fighting cocks, the cathedrals, they constitute a continuous, coherent and formidable oeuvre. Never seeing the new and innovative as a threat, he was quite prepared to ruffle feathers whenever he felt it to be necessary, albeit this would be accomplished with elegance and a mischievous glint in his eye.

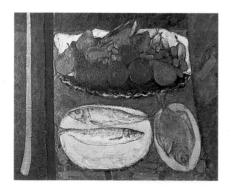

CHAPTER EIGHT

WHEN HE BECAME HEAD OF THE PAINTING SCHOOL IN 1960 PHILIPSON inherited trouble. For some time he had been conscious of his generation's lost war years putting extra age-distance between master and pupil, but at 43 he was still young for the job. Student unrest in universities and colleges all over Britain was already simmering but took some time to come to the boil. They bucked the system, the curriculum and staff attitudes, demanded better conditions, grants and facilities. Sandy Moffat, now head of the painting school at Glasgow School of Art and a distinguished Scottish painter, arrived as a student at ECA just when Philipson was promoted. Recognised as one of the 60s "revolutionaries" alongside his friend John Bellany, his memoir of student days, and of Philipson as head of school, is tempered by hindsight:

> I had no contact with him until second year when I showed one of my Alan Davie/Jackson Pollock paintings in an exhibition in the Sculpture Court. The very next day I was dragged out of class to be given a "severe dressing down." If I continued on this path, I was told – running before walking – I would be dismissed from the college. (Gillies told me not to worry about Robin at this stage).

> After that, subsequent meetings were a little tense – but there were words of encouragement for a number of my still-life paintings. However, at the beginning of my third year things turned nasty again. I embarked upon a Cubist/African/Picasso still-life (John Bellany has this in his collection). When Philipson saw what I was doing he called Bob Callender, my class tutor, into the corridor and asked why he hadn't put a stop to what I was doing. I could hear them shouting at each other outside the studio. Bob argued that it was a good painting and that I had every right to attempt such a thing. And so on. This kind of struggle continued all through my third and fourth years – incidents too numerous and petty to mention.

> Looking back over that period now, I can only ponder about all of these things… Philipson was, after all, a Scottish painter who knew Kokoschka and Beckmann; he had fought against fascism and was an expressive figurative painter and humanist. All of these things were what I *wanted* for painting. Where did it all go wrong? Why didn't we see eye to eye on all of these issues? There was about Philipson in those days the manner of the ex-army officer – autocratic and given to issuing orders. All of this was anathema to me and to a lot of my generation. We were sick to the teeth of "war heroes" and the like, telling us that we were a bunch of saps, and so on. I had been attracted to the ideal of art as a revolutionary/radical force in society – something capable of changing all of the worst aspects of humanity, and because the art world seemed a genuinely

democratic community, where we would all work together as equals. Philipson seemed to stand for the opposite – an elitist, pseudo-aristocrat, with no interest at all in "the struggle." This was not only a struggle about socialist ideals, but also a battle for Scottish culture and art – for our national soul, if you like. During my student years I first met MacDiarmid and became friendly with Norman MacCaig. Those poets along with Sydney Goodsir Smith and Sorley MacLean presented a vital alternative to what seemed the "bourgeois" world of Scottish (RSA) painting. Their ability to deal with the reality of Scottish issues in an imaginative and creative way seemed far more valid than the current kind of established Scottish painting – represented of course, more than anyone else, by Robin Philipson, the artistic "dandy."

Although I'm no great admirer of Robin's later work I now concede that he was a considerable force for good in many ways. He certainly believed that being an artist was a very serious business indeed, and that art should aspire to do all sorts of noble things. His ideas or belief in intuitive or spontaneous acts was obviously based on the assumption that before a painter could become properly expressive and fluent, a certain amount of basic work had to be accomplished first of all. I think too, for all his establishment posturing, he wanted and intended his art to encompass the idea of change and revolution – in the widest sense – that an understanding of the creative and aesthetic would improve and enrich people. He had a mission.

Robin put the fear of death into his contemporaries and his staff. He was I think mystified why this didn't happen to myself or John Bellany. He couldn't handle it when we simply stood up to him. He certainly couldn't understand our wish to take painting on to the streets [during the Edinburgh Festival of 1963 Moffat and Bellany hung their paintings on railings in the city centre]. At the end of the day I have to thank him for those early days of opposition, because in order to stand up to him it was necessary for me to become just as serious and committed – and work as hard as I could to become a good painter.

Moffat and Philipson made their peace, certainly by the 70s when Moffat had established himself as an accomplished portraitist, and even more so in the 80s when Moffat played such a major role as a teacher in the emergence of the "new" Glasgow Boys. Bellany and Philipson established a deep personal friendship which enriched both their lives.

John Houston was a member of staff at ECA in the 60s and thinks, in retrospect, that too much is made of the student troubles. "It was natural for young people to question the accepted order. They'd been taught that at school. They reacted against what they thought was the airy-fairy stuff of the past. They wanted to paint the working man, to reflect the age they were living in. If it wasn't that, it would have been something else. When we came into school in the mornings we were handed left-wing leaflets, usually by Alan Bold having a go at Robin and Jimmy Cumming – they were the principal targets. It has always struck me as slightly unfair that the college was saddled with that revolutionary reputation. People like John Bellany got every prize and every scholarship it was possible to give a student."

Philipson had four London exhibitions in the 60s, three with the Scottish Gallery, and was included in several important group shows of Scottish and British painting in this country and abroad. His work was exhibited in Warsaw in 1967 following a visit he had made to the Polish city in 1964. That year he had a gall-bladder operation followed by an attack of acute pancreatitis, the first of many life-threatening illnesses he would now endure. In 1965 he was elected to the Royal Fine Art Commission for Scotland, won the Leverhulme Travelling Award, and was made a Fellow of the Royal Society of Artists.

The public figure co-existed quite happily with the private man. One day in 1965 he took himself to the cinema, as he often did, as an escapist diversion. The film was *King and Country*, Joseph Losey's adaptation of the First World War stage drama *Hump* by John Wilson. Tom Courtenay plays the part of a young private soldier who is court martialled and shot for desertion – "cowardice," as the army implied – in the face of the most terrifying battles of modern times. Philipson was moved to compassion and anger by Losey's stark and graphic treatment of a savage story. The film fertilised an idea that had been lying dormant for some time and launched him on a new theme, a sequence of trench-war pictures which would gather up other strands of his

work – rose windows, crucifixions, cock fights, "used" women who became the first of many Philipson "floosies" – and incorporate them in compositions showing skeins of men going into action in sombre friezes. He had been born during that war, his childhood and young life reverberated with its aftermath of widows and limbless survivors and crosses studded with the names of the dead on every village green. He had something he wanted to say about war, an obscenity he had seen for himself. He experimented with several paintings of executions – bleak compositions with figures, often crudely drawn and reduced to crusty blobs, slumped dead at stakes with target markers pinned to their chests. The sequence ranged through these explicit images to two enigmatic paintings called *Never Mind*, both begun in 1965 and one of them not completed until 1984, which are dominated by spare monochromatic studies of an executed soldier overseen by a slightly caricatured portrait of an officer, who might have fought with Wellington, and seeming to echo Voltaire's jibe about the English hanging their admirals *"pour encourager les autres." Stone the Crows* is the most innovative and descriptive of the single-panel war paintings. It is a square composed of five horizontal narrative bands, bordered by what seem to be the sprocket-holes of film footage. The overall effect at the centre is of a yellowing montage of men with fixed bayonets running, diving, crawling into no-man's-land – as realistic as faded old sepia photographs. Below them is an expressionist tumult of men, horses and vehicles fighting their way through the stinking morass of Flanders mud. The painting takes its title – the slang expletive for astonishment – from the top band, in which a row of dead crows strung along a fence (*pour encourager les autres* again?) is recipro

"Stone the Crows"

cated by the bodies of dead soldiers snagged in similar attitudes on barbed wire defences. The secular sermon, for as such I will always see it, is terminated at the base of the picture by the candyfloss pink glow surrounding a reclining nude, a voluptuous metaphor for all the de Maupassant whores who have plied their trade in the "comfort stations," selling sex and solace to the survivors of battle throughout history.

As a deliberate contrast to the lustrous glazes of his cathedral interiors and rose windows, built up over months of rotation on the easel, the war pictures were painted in bursts of furious activity, with vinyl toluene replacing linseed oil as a medium. "I tried," he said, "to get a more than usual mattness, using a lifeless, inert paint, to suggest the dullness of earth itself, the earthiness of the trenches and no-man's-land, and men in their thousands dying and becoming earth themselves." While the toluene was still tacky he increased the dullness by dusting on pure pigment. According to Colin Thomson "a surface that was shiny with varnish was protected – safe – and, for Robin, it was dead. Exactly this kind of marriage between paint and subject had become fundamental to his way of working."

There were several other major paintings in this period of intense exploration and activity. *Golgotha*, a polyptych study for an altarpiece, is – in its concept and scale – one of the most extraordinary watercolour paintings ever attempted. Its central panel is a crucifixion, flanked by two hinged and detachable wings painted back and front. Beneath is a seven-panel predella. Instead of crucified thieves alongside the central Christ figure there are two men bound to stakes, one alive the other dead. The central panel of the predella is a cock fight. As if he were trying to push himself to some physical limit and expand his ideas to monumental proportions the submissions for his Scottish Gallery 1965 Festival exhibition included *Golgotha*, a large triptych *The Way to Eternity* and another polyptych, probably the most challenging composition he ever attempted, *Defenders of the Realm*. At one level this is a startling war memorial, an orchestrated, abstracted chronicle of visual expression in rich oil and toluene, a celebration of victory and a hosanna for deliverance. A square central panel is bracketed by two narrower wing panels, surmounting a predella made up of five small squares. It is not the only Philipson painting which, consciously or unconsciously, suggests Jungian symbolism as its energetic source. The concept of the mandala – a pictorial image of the universe and a symbol of self which is used in the Buddhist and Hindu meditation process – depends for its wholeness and symmetry, the path to the psychic centre, on the harmony one can achieve in oneself. *Defenders of the Realm* reiterates colour and texture, moving in and out of step with itself. Its polyphonic diversity and symphonic unity, its call and response in tone and time, all of this movement, beauty and emotion is gathered up and resolved at its central core.

A decade which had seen him increasing his popularity as a decorative painter, establishing himself in London, elected secretary of the RSA and to the Council of the Edinburgh Festival Society, ended with his work being shown in New York alongside other Scottish painters.

JOHN HOUSTON – Coming out of that wee spat with Sandy Moffat broadened him out. He was never again quite as dictatorial with the students. He learned to laugh things off.

SANDY MOFFAT – I still admire Philipson's early paintings (up to around 1960) – his Kokoschka period. These are marvellous things – the Edinburgh paintings for example, turbulent, fluent, and highly charged – wonderful pictures. After this I feel, the paintings become more and more contrived, often striking false notes – expertly manufactured, of course, but ultimately "chocolate box." Occasionally a perfect little watercolour would slip through, a nude, a flower piece, painted from the heart and without all the pomp and affectation of his grander works, and these awful rose windows.

ROBERT CALLENDER – We had lots of bother. "CALLENDER," he'd shriek, "in here!" And I'd get another dressing-down and argue back. Always about student work. Why was I allowing them to do this and that. It got quite physical at times. But I tell you this, he'd rant and rave at you inside the school, but if anybody breathed a word against you outside the school he'd be the first to spring to your defence. He ran the place the way he thought it ought to be and it started to go to hell as soon as he left.

WILLIAM BAILLIE – The one thing we had absolutely in common was a ridiculous sense of humour. I think we were opposites. He could get terribly worked up and it takes me a long time. I'm much steadier. He liked to bounce things off me because he knew I wasn't going to get up to ninety about it. He once called me a thermometer. It was a phrase he used to Gillies – "if you have a word with Bill Baillie he'll give you the temperature of certain college situations." But our humour was a great joy, just being completely madcap, often about quite serious issues. His sister always said to my wife that I was more of a brother to Robin than a friend. I was very fond of him, but he could be extremely difficult. We had serious disagreements, but I was always able to go to Robin and say I thought he was wrong. He would take it from me, but with other people it didn't work out at all. He could be very articulate when angry, talking rat-tat-tat, dressing people down, and you never knew when that side of him was going to pop up. And there's no doubt that, as his health deteriorated, he became more volatile.

JACK FIRTH – Anyone who thought he was foppish didn't know the man – elegant, consciously stylish in a manner more common in his day, fastidiously individual – but foppish, never. When I hear people describing him as peevish, a volatile prima donna, insensitive to all the massive problems of all those student geniuses whose sensibilities were offended by his "officer class" manners, his dismissal of their natural hatred of "war heroes"... Oh, how my heart bleeds for them! I think those people who have made a lot of mileage out of their courageous defiance of authority owe Robin a posthumous apology.

Philipson and Baillie on a Trip to Venice

CHAPTER NINE

IN THE SPRING OF 1970 THE SCOTTISH ARTS COUNCIL GAVE PHILIPSON his first major solo public exhibition and toured it in Scotland and the north of England. *Cockfight Rosewindow* was an imaginative and dramatic concept by William Buchanan, at that time the Arts Council's visual arts director in Scotland. The exhibition began its life in Edinburgh, travelled to Sunderland and Newcastle, then came back over the border to Milngavie, Aberdeen, Greenock and Glasgow. Almost 100 paintings based on these two familiar themes produced a vivid pageant of movement and colour, serenity and savagery. The themes complemented each other in juxtaposition, on occasion became potently interwoven, and in a few canvases incorporated images from other painting series. The pictures were gathered together from national and municipal collections as well as Philipson's many private admirers. It is interesting that at the end of his life the artist did not have a single example of the cock fight or rose window series in his personal collection.

In his catalogue essay Buchanan says: "We cannot escape asking why these two themes in particular have interested him so

"That other Christmas"

deeply. I suggest that somehow they allowed the artist to express emotions which were present at a particular time in his life. How far this suggestion can be proved, what conclusion can be drawn from it, and many other questions, can best be considered... in front of the paintings themselves." He went on to quote a set of rules for creative activity (music, painting, writing) formulated by the scientist Desmond Morris (himself a surrealist painter), which he had outlined in his recently published best-seller *The Naked Ape*.

1 you shall investigate the unfamiliar until it has become familiar; 2. you shall impose rhythmic repetition on the familiar; 3. you shall vary this repetition in as many ways as possible; 4. you shall select the most satisfying of these variations and develop them at the expense of others; 5. you shall combine and recombine these variations one with another; 6. and you shall do all this for its own sake, as an end in itself.

"By these rules," said Buchanan, "Robin Philipson must be the archetypal artist." Writing in *The Daily Telegraph* at this time the critic Terence Mullaly said: "It is now inescapable that Robin Philipson is a commanding figure in the art of the 20th century." *Cockfight Rosewindow* was complemented across the River Forth – as part of the Dunfermline Festival of that year – by the artist's first major retrospective exhibition, and so, for some weeks in the spring of 1970, lowland Scotland had the first chance to see an extensive review of the artist's work, spanning 20 years. The Scottish Gallery promoted him with yet another Edinburgh Festival show, which began to extend the development of an important new theme – *Waiting Women* and the more thoroughly investigated *Women Observed*. That year also saw him plucking many new chords on the *Threnody* theme and the first of a series of paintings hitched to George Bruce's suggestion of a generic title, *Humankind*. "All kind involving humankind was what we both meant," Philipson explained. "George hoped that one word would take the viewer into the painting's heart." These "state of the world" essays, expressing humility, concern and wonder, were often fragmented on the canvas to reiterate differing statements on the same subject. Ever since his visit to Warsaw in 1964, when he had long discussions on the subject with a fellow-painter, he had experimented with the device of dividing the picture space into separate panels, opening up vertical and horizontal corridors, introducing his chromatic ladders and rainbows to define borders, to suggest that here one world starts and there another one ends, yet preserving the human condition – its comedy and tragedy, paradox and mystery – as an inevitable unity.

Humankind began with a painting of a white girl and a black boy which was exhibited and sold. The artist never saw it again. "It must have been of a very low order," he said, "because I remember nothing else about it. It didn't work. Time and time again I proved that the confrontation had to be the other way round." It was a theme that "floated in" from nowhere, like the cock fights, but unlike rose windows, cathedrals, kings and jesters, crucifixions, women observed and the war pictures, all of which had been carefully considered and researched. The black girl and white boy had an almost mystical provenance.

> I'd been giving a lecture in Duns or somewhere, and I was motoring back through the Borders on this late autumn evening in an old truck. There was a ditch running alongside the road, full of straw and grass, and suddenly, for no reason whatsoever, suddenly there was a black girl lying there. I knew there was no reality to this, none whatsoever, and I thought, what an extraordinary experience. And in my head I took it a stage further and thought, if I had been 20 or 30 years of age I might have stopped the car, got out and raped her. And as I realised the dreadful enormity of that thought, the illusion of the girl travelled along the road with me as the truck kept moving. The vision vanished of course, but left me with the compulsion to paint a series of pictures about the awful enigma of a black girl and white boy, occasionally on the periphery of sex, but determined not to be involved in it, part of the whole human scene, caught up in all kinds of human circumstance, where interiors and exteriors became very elaborate and different, but no matter where I put them, no matter the situation they are in, there is an intense longing and guilt, and the sense of the forbidden, and the prospect of penance and punishment. It's a deep and terrible fascination, a spontaneous and profound mystery which stays with me. Even now, I don't think I've exhausted that theme. For one thing, I think it has great intellectual beauty, just the thought of it. I had seen naked native girls of incredible beauty, slender, moving about performing menial tasks unaware of their sexuality, certainly oblivious to the sexual and racial polarity of the situation. But if you're going to address that in a painting it has to come into it straight, blatantly, ferociously and immediately. Then it's the other things that you add that soften, qualify, extenuate and properly place in the history of our minds. That's my job. That's what I have to try and do.

In a catalogue commentary for the Scottish Gallery 1970 Festival show William Buchanan talks about the animals which invariably attend the couple. "A monkey or ape appears in many of these paintings – most powerfully of all in that showing an ape howling as the boy and girl embrace. Horses, cocks and bulls which we know already lurk in the artist's private zoological garden are now joined by less noble companions. Yet when, as happens in the tiniest watercolour, the black girl and the white boy lie in the closest embrace the artist refers not to animal lust but makes his comment by placing above them a yellow rose."

There is little doubt that the erotic frisson of the black girl/white boy paintings and pastels made them commercially

popular. Philipson admitted that he enjoyed creating the sexual parody of *Women Observed* in all their manifestations. "London kept teasing me to bring down some more ladies." These naked or partially draped figures – faceless, apparently loitering with intent, often diffused in a blush of pigment, sometimes the tantalising subject of the painting or merely hovering on its peripheries, amused and diverted him. Demure on a *chaise-longue* or brazenly posturing, ambiguously propositioning or classically aloof, they might be playing out the age-old conundrum of the madonna-whore – seen by some as Delacroix odalisques, by others as shameless floosies. William Hardie says Philipson's *demi-mondaines*, painted by a man whose natural gifts include "a remarkable power of suggestion and description," suggest that the roles of man as aggressor and woman as victim "are at the root of the war of the sexes and perhaps also at the root of war *tout court*." Lilian Browse dismisses the notion, frequently suggested, that these women are intended to be objects of sexual titillation. "Robin, like most artists, much appreciated the female nude. Paintings of nudes appear throughout his work and in the series of *Women Observed* many have seen them as brothels. I cannot accept this interpretation of such tranquil and detached canvases, for very rarely do they show any base interest in sex." Duncan Macmillan talks about the disturbing effect of the violence or implied violence of *Women Observed* "in which two women naked, or partly dressed in one panel of a diptych are apparently watched by snarling dogs in the other, but the artist remains curiously detached."

By this time Philipson was so confident in his choice of subject matter that, with the exception of landscape, he found something

to fuel his imagination wherever he turned his head. Knowing the effects he wished to create – like a stage director marshalling his technical accomplices – he had become even more engrossed in experiments with materials and method. Huge sheets of paper for watercolour panels needed huge sheets of plate glass to keep them wet. Concerned about the stability of colour and its permanence he forsook linseed oil as a painting medium and went back to Cennini to refine turpentine by leaving it in saucers in the sun. Joan Eardley had taught him how to achieve the most saturated colour by drawing his pastels on the fine tooth of French sandpaper. A rich bitter yellow – Indian Yellow – he often used was originally created by suspending pigment in the urine of oxen. His blues and greens, pinks and reds became more idiosyncratic and specific. If some of his lustrous impasto looked as if it might shine in the dark the matt passages produced by vinyl toluene retreated into an opaque limbo. A cock fight was painted in oil and gold leaf on leather. American pop art introduced many new materials; he tried them all and rejected most of them. One of the most important innovations was the introduction of patches of Japanese paper, pressed into oil pigment while it was still wet, then painted over in thin glazes and integrated with surrounding textures to create illusions of reverberating depth. Glazes, and his clever use of their transparent alchemy, became a favorite device throughout the rest of his career.

Not content with the effects he could conjure on the surface of his paintings Philipson wanted to heighten the radiance of his colour by giving it actual depth. He found himself approaching a bare canvas with an entirely different attitude. After preparing the ground he would normally "go at it," impulsively, with broad gestural flourish, the results of which might remain and grow or get scrubbed out, or would be altered and developed in another mode. Now, as often as he could, he approached the easel with a clear sight of his intentions, almost as if he could project his vision of the completed painting on to the bare canvas. This forethought was vital, because in his new method the underpainting – some of which might be allowed to glow through – was made up of a grid of small squares of pure colour, feathered into each other at the edges, and preselected in tone and hue so that they would correspond with the final scheme he saw so vividly in his imagination.

There is no doubt that Philipson's preoccupation with *matière* and his willingness to talk about his methods and discoveries to colleagues and friends contributed to a suspicion that he had become more interested in substance than spirit in his painting.

John Houston, who had spent so many years at ECA with him, thought that view went too far, but believes that sometimes the method of achieving the image was too fussy. "Lots of people loved his involved descriptions, other painters listened to him and followed his lead. I remember being bamboozled by them. In a way it just seemed to be technique for its own sake. I always felt that when he was most direct he was at his strongest – his big watercolours, the late small ones, and of course his pastels. I didn't like to have to fight through all these blocks of paint which seemed to be almost sculptural – they became the image and got in the way of his drawing. He could draw in the most direct and powerful way, and he was a very strong designer, and didn't need all that icing on the cake. Later in life he came back to a much simpler kind of painting, less involved, even in the oils, and he was all the better for that."

In 1971 I made a 30-minute film for my *Scope* art series on BBC television of Philipson at work. He was a reluctant subject. This master of public address which he delivered with aplomb – in an off-the-cuff manner which belied his hours of preparation – distrusted his tongue's ability to do his wits justice in the artificial spontaneity of a television interview. With great courtesy he had turned me down several times, but I made one last plea and he promised to reconsider. I had been out of my office for over an hour, and when I returned my young assistant (who is now my wife) was arranging a filming schedule with him on the telephone. Robin this and Robin that, and yes, we'd be with him a week on Monday. He had called to say he had finally decided against the project, but after an hour of earnest blandishment the charmer had been charmed. In the course of an industrious week we explored his studio, his palettes, work on the walls and finished paintings on their way to a show. Robin judged a film crew's appetites perfectly by keeping up a constant flow of bacon butties, and on the last day painted from scratch a spectacular watercolour that embraced a black girl in a gothic arch, an exploding rose window, and a chorus of nubile naked women. He often recalled the *volte face* that had induced the programme, the fun we had making it, and never failed to include it in any survey of his professional life.

In the autumn of 1972, rewarded for years of leadership and accomplished management at ECA, Philipson set out on a 12-month sabbatical study. His marriage to Thora Clyne was still intact but his travelling companion on the way to Greece was Diana Pollock, a friend and former secretary of the college principal. At Boulogne, on the first leg of the journey, he became very ill and was admitted to hospital. Cancer of the colon was discovered and he was operated on immediately. Thora arrived from Scotland and for almost three months the two women attended him in hospital. "It was all a bit delicate," he told me. "In a crisis like that though, when people are stretched to their limits and caught up in such stress, it's amazing how you see the best of them, they get priorities right." Within a month of his surgery he was drawing day-by-day the flowers and "get well" cards by his

A bedside painting from Boulogne

bedside. The week before he came home he spent some time sketching in the countryside. *Boulogne And After*, a show of these works "of modest character and having little or no drama," was mounted at the Scottish Gallery in 1973. Some of these felt pen and crayon drawings and watercolours were exquisite in their formal simplicity. That year, slowly recovering his health, he was elected an Associate of the Royal Academy and achieved the great distinction of being elected President of the Royal Scottish Academy.

WILLIAM BAILLIE — His contribution to the Academy was outstanding. He brought the student exhibition, which is now such a success, under our roof. At the time of his election there was a lot of hostility towards the RSA. We were fortunate to have someone as articulate as Robin, a painter of stature, to withstand the flak, to argue for us so lucidly, and fly the Academy's flag. He knew the RSA had to get up off its backside and stop behaving like a small club, tell the country what we were about and broadcast what we were doing. He was a charming personality, a bit of a showman — and the last to deny it — and he revelled in the big occasion.

TERENCE MULLALY – He is a magician of the brush; in his hands oil paint is a thing of delight, colour appeals directly to the senses, and before his work is an almost tangible sense of physical well being. This ability to heighten the viewer's awareness of his own existence, to cast aside material preoccupations, in fact all the trivia that pass for life, is one of the touchstones of art that continues to move man… in an age when the arts have been threatened both by extravagant anarchy and cold intellectualism, leading to what has been aptly called minimal art, Philipson has charmed and sometimes ravished the senses and has also rewarded the mind.

DOUGLAS HALL (1994) – I am sure he was sensitive enough to know that I was not a fervent admirer of his painting. It must be twenty-five years since I wrote an introduction to a show of his at Aitken Dott's, and it was by no means unflattering, but it was never to be repeated.

It was an unspoken fact between us that the bulk of the Philipsons in the [SNGMA] Collection came from [the bequest of] Robbie Scott-Hay. I think in fact that the two major works I did buy – the 1960s watercolour triptych *The Burning*, and the big sea piece of the 1980s – showed him at his best, but I suspect he felt that, as they were not wholly typical, it implied a judgement on his more ordinary work.

Robin was too big a man to be treated as a figurehead or as some simple paragon without internal contradictions. Given his humanity and benign nature one cannot doubt that his grim themes were hateful to him, and it is an enigma to me that he could not unleash his emotions about them. It is almost as if he felt that to do so would be to betray something essential in the school of painting (and of feeling) he had given his allegiance to.

JOHN HOUSTON – I think he probably took the experimental technical side too far. And of course I've recently seen some paintings in a hell of a state. Physically, in at least two of them, there's a lot of cracking already going on, and I wonder about quite a number from certain periods. Then the charm thing… Some people never got on with him. Quite a number fell out and never got over it. Peter Collins is still very bitter. Bob Callender and Robin never really hit it off, and one or two other people. Robin's charm didn't really work on them.

SIR ANTHONY WHEELER – In my view he was an outstanding colourist and absolute master of his own particular "glazing" technique. I would think that this creative skill alone would establish for him a unique place in 20th-century Scottish painting. He was a fine watercolourist but unfortunately he tended to limit his output in this field, largely I think because he considered that his watercolour technique took such a long time.

JUDITH BUMPUS – Philipson was as subtly contradictory as were the themes he dealt with: beauty (a word he was not afraid to use) and ugliness, pleasure and suffering, the spirit and the flesh, tolerance and prejudice. To all the world a gregarious and outgoing personality, he was, on his own admission, a loner and a dreamer. In the studio it was the solitary ebb and flow of emotion, working hand-in-hand with brush and paint, that eventually came up with the expressive and meaningful image.

WILLIAM BUCHANAN – One characteristic of Philipson's art is the balancing of one theme with another. So, for each forbidden sensual pleasure there is ensuing penance – expressed in the series of paintings of a crucifixion, where a flayed and twisted figure is nailed face inwards to the cross.

JOHN HOUSTON – He had a large circle of friends and loved parties – a leading light in the college revels, loved dressing up. He drew a 35-foot high, Soutine-like pastry cook and we made it up out of brown paper and painted it all through the night. I was his assistant. He had no interest in sport or politics. I never heard him express a political opinion in his life. For somebody who loved food as much as he did, the big surprise was his appetite for potatoes. If Robin was coming you always added another 20 to the pot. He was mad about potatoes.

JACK FIRTH – I think sometimes of the university student – son of a friend of Robin's and mine – who occasionally met Robin on a tramcar going up Frederick Street to Chambers Street. Impoverished as students always are, after he had ended his journey the young man used to find that he had unaccountably acquired a £5 note in his jacket pocket. Nothing was ever said.

"Arena"

CHAPTER TEN

PHILIPSON WORE HIS ROLE AS PRESIDENT OF THE ROYAL SCOTTISH Academy like an ermine mantle. Elected by his peers, already distinguished by reputation as artist, teacher and administrator, showered by appointments and awards, he could have sat back at the age of 56, held court and basked in the social afterglow. Edinburgh is that kind of city, the RSA that kind of body. And he made it obvious that he enjoyed the pomp of a royal visit to the annual exhibition, the opening of a major Festival show when half the world seemed to camp on the capital's doorstep, the dressing-up, the courteous public performance he could turn on with such easy charm. Douglas Hall, as keeper of the Scottish National Gallery of Modern Art, observed him on many occasions: "Robin by his mere presence gave a grace and delicacy to an otherwise stodgy gathering. No wonder he was in demand." But Philipson took his presidential responsibilities seriously, lobbied earnestly to banish some of the RSA's stuffy Victorian attitudes which discouraged the participation of Scotland's younger painters, and – most strenuously – did everything he could to end a tedious and artificial schism between Edinburgh and Glasgow. This social and cultural rift between the cities has existed for over a century. It is a good-natured flyte on the whole, invigorated by many barbed jokes and satirical jibes, but in the artistic communities east and west, real animosity and envy, false pride and cultivated huffs, exaggerated the divide.

Philipson went out of his way to build bridges, persuade west of Scotland painters in particular that the Academy, as a national institution, would be enriched by their involvement in its affairs. He is remembered as the most successful PRSA in the second half of the century. James Morrison amplifies his opinion – "in my time he was the best" – by singling out Philipson's determination to encourage the election of painters furth of Edinburgh.

> I remember him saying most pointedly at an RSA assembly, "I think the Edinburgh-Glasgow thing is dead." He had a wholly beneficial influence on painting in Scotland. It was typical that, when retiring from the Presidency, and he had to choose a painter to paint his portrait for the Academy, he chose David Donaldson, the essential Glasgow painter, and a doughty defender of the west in Edinburgh.

The torrent of work that flowed from Philipson in the 60s abated only slightly in the 70s. If advancing age, some physical infirmity and an enormous burden of college and public duties constrained his painting hours it was apparent only in the absence of new major themes and fewer experimental works on a massive scale. Threnody throbbed on. He had by no means worked off his enthusiasm for cathedral interiors, Mexican altars and crucifixions. His interest in the polarity of black and white was extended to studies of zebras. Ambitious multi-image works with titles like *Gethsemane* and *Iconostasis* emerged alongside more modest, but nevertheless dynamic departures like *The Whisper* and *Barking Dog*. Cardinal figures, drenched in red, harked back to the reign of Philipson pageantry, kings and jesters and armoured knights. A heartfelt *Homage to Gillies* appeared as a construct of powerful images in a vertical triptych. His women still teased and loitered, and *Men Observed* began to hover in various guises. He returned to scenes of summer which Kokoschka had once inspired. There was even an occasional cock fight. He had three major solo shows in London and Edinburgh during the decade, an exhibition of cathedral paintings in Elgin, and another retrospective in Stirling. He travelled to Belgrade and visited Kenya and South Africa on an English Speaking Union scholarship. His marriage to Thora Clyne was dissolved in 1975. The following year he married Diana Pollock – the year the Queen knighted him for his services to the arts in Scotland.

By the end of the decade he was "as decorated as a Christmas tree," held more public appointments than any man should be asked to devote his valuable time and energy to, yet lost none of his voracious appetite for work. He concerned himself less with technical experiment and began to confine himself to refining what he had learned about materials and occasionally re-inventing his palette to suit new moods and subjects. Meantime, as ever, "I didn't go out looking for ideas for a painting – they came to me." And when they did they usually went on the back-burner of his mind, for years sometimes, but in any event not before he had challenged their validity – as decoration, as his kind of visual poetry, as commentary on the human condition. The time would come, however, when he thought the process of gestation was over; he was ready to set out on some fresh adventure and, as he admitted, approached the fresh canvas in a state of trepidation and anticipation.

> I think in the making of images the actual quality of the action is important. I enjoy superlatively-placed paint – like in a Van Gogh – each brushstroke. When I'm working I also enjoy in my humble way the rough and tumble of this bloody stuff that will not do as it's told. You want to create an image, whether it's an animal, a human figure, or whatever, or a passage of paint that has no apparent relevance until you make it relevant, and relevant doesn't mean you make it literal – far from it, in fact. So you get this opportunity for play, for play and sideplay, and of course you realise eventually that you've given yourself almost too much to hold together. The emotional tension is almost unbearable. And it's at that point you have to be very, very careful. You can't get carried away and allow this excitement to

turn into extravagant, gestural play just for the sake of it. When you do, if you do, you know perfectly well you're getting into trouble. And sometimes you can't bear it, so you go on putting the stuff on, knowing that, whatever happens, you'll have to come to the studio the next day to scrape it all off while it's still wet.

It's the most desperately lonely business. I sometimes dread going to that studio. I get myself there without thinking, just get there, and light the gas fire and put my easel in the right position. I can't remember any day I've gone there enthusiastic about what I was going to do – you have to start work and believe that the excitement will come later in the day. But the idea of losing what you had yesterday, of ruining a hard day's work, is often so strong you begin to feel, oh lord, I better leave this until tomorrow.

We sometimes say of our work – "that one painted itself," and of course it didn't, but that feeling about it is legitimate, because some special facility with the paint and the enormous psychological build up within oneself came together that day. It's a complete mystery, but it begins to be an understandable mystery if you take the trouble to dig deep and find out, if you can, the origins of your imagery, where it might have sprung from. I have often thought of a man like Francis Bacon, who could go on painting virtually the same image in the same classical framelike format, then being able to push in that moment of magic that makes each painting not only different, but different in the most terrifying way. That's what the mystery is about really, and it's very exciting.

Then if you think of someone like Lucien Freud, his very curious and painstaking vision, as if he were writing down every moment of his personal reaction to flesh. He knows the normal response will be unpleasant. You don't get flesh washed-out like that except in peo-

The Secret Garden

ple who are rather poorly. But it's his way of seeing a kind of reality – and a kind of mortality as well. I often wonder whether he frames it in the right psychological way… if one took away the essence of *skinness* – you know, the sense of skin dying even as it lives – I wonder what one would be left with? Not a lot, maybe. Yet you feel that he has taken that extra stride, that bloody great push in the back that puts you into a new aura, where you're terribly lost, don't quite know what you're going to do, yet feel you have the authority of portent and the capacity to step into the future. You're not the old lady dressed up in a circus tent and reading palms, but you allow your ignorance and awareness to run the whole gamut of curiousity. In many ways the prospect of the future is terrifying. I could be very easily terrified, even to the point of wanting to give up.

I would love to get more of this into my work – more mystery and wonder and fear – but so far I feel I have failed. You keep saying to yourself, well that small miracle which is just round the corner will do it, and that's when you resort to excuses about the problems of making paint do what it's told. The truth is that paint isn't difficult to handle. It's the scale of the mystery, and the opportunity for error, and your own ineptness in creating that visionary space you would like to enter in the last quarter of a painting's development. That's when you take the extra stride, need the shove in the back.

In 1981 he had a happy event thrust upon him – in London he was elected an Honorary Royal Academician. He nervously participated in the creation of another, when he and Diana adopted a baby boy, Jasper, who would bring them great joy, and reveal to

Robin that even at 64 he had a gift for fatherhood. His old friends were, to say the least, amazed. He confessed to me that he had approached the expansion of his happy and stable five-year-old marriage, into the unknown territory of a family unit, with some misgivings. At his age what kind of father would he make, how much might it disrupt his professional life, and how adequately could he deal with all the responsibilities of being a parent? He was on the brink of retirement from ECA and looking forward to the first opportunity life had offered him to spend all his working hours painting. Despite his remarkable commercial success as a painter he was not a rich man. Generous to a fault, he also enjoyed spending money, and after his divorce there had been additional drains on his finances. "All my life," he said apropos of nothing at all during one of our conversations, "I've been afraid of being poor." With some coaxing he added: "It would get in the way of my work. I wouldn't be able to do the things I wanted to do. But I know that as an individual I wouldn't have the character to face the ignominy. I don't dwell on it, it isn't a recurring nightmare, but I'm aware of it lurking away, it's always there."

I suggested that his ECA salary and constant commercial sales must have been able to support a very comfortable lifestyle, well beyond his dreams. "My parents were quite poor. They had been more comfortably off, but for various reasons that changed, and school fees for me and my sister made matters worse. My fear of poverty came from watching them worry about money – there just wasn't enough. Nobody ever knew, of course, because my mother and father were wizards, not at concealing, but at always looking nice, always having a good table, and possessing a few very beautiful things from a time when they weren't so poor. I probably did say to myself, damn it, that's not going to happen to me. But there's no connection between that and any attempt on my part to sell pictures. I've been very lucky to sell so well, especially since I couldn't imagine anyone wanting to live with so many of them."

Philipson retired, as planned, in 1981. More than anything else he missed the perquisite of his magnificent college studio and the devoted attendance of skilled technicians. He had to make do with a do-it-yourself studio at home. The following year he demitted office as PRSA and gathered in even more time for the planned painting campaign of his mature years. His 1983 Festival show at the Scottish Gallery reflected this refreshed impetus. He had traversed the output of over 30 years as a professional painter; assessed success and diagnosed failure; reconsidered the sheer hedonism of so much colour and rejected complexity when he felt bold enough to go for a more brutal monochromatic image. Above all, he had ranged around the fringes of his canvases to

snap up – like Autolycus – the unconsidered trifles of his imagination and develop them into more substantial statements.

Two paintings of *The Covering Sea* dipped into some of the energy and lithe expressionism of his homage to Kokoschka. A massive triptych *Presentation* postulated the damnation of mankind in the person of a fallen Eve – stark sleaze up against Sanderson wallpaper, an all-embracing glimpse of the voyeur's heaven and hell. In a hunt sequence his lifelong love of the elegance of horses gave a keener, contrapuntal edge to his curiosity about male behaviour. A self-portrait in a squiffy straw hat is a quizzical confrontation framed within the boundaries of his own easel. No sooner had people recoiled – as they did – from the snarling ferocity of a mangy pariah dog, sculpted (so heavy was the crude impasto) on a four-foot-square canvas, than they were seduced by *Poppies on a Blue Ground*, the first of many choreographed, large-scale paintings of these fragile blooms which he set to his own dynamic music for the rest of his life.

That 1983 Scottish Gallery show of 64 works was, as intended, a landmark – and was recognised as such. The critic Mary Rose Beaumont hailed it as "an outstanding demonstration of all that is best in Scottish art… Philipson has dared much in these paintings: they are the work of a man who has meditated profoundly about the nature of art and of an artist with a supreme concern about the meaning of life."

London's appetite for his work increased and buyers' tastes went well beyond sensual response to his mysterious houris, and the decorative appeal of his still-lifes and ornate church interiors. He had built up a formidable and sophisticated following in Cork Street. In 1985 the family welcomed an adopted baby girl, Rebecca, and as Phyllis Gwilliam says: "He really enjoyed these

children. I don't think he had any idea what to expect. He was not just surprised but, bound up with the happiness he shared with Diana, he discovered a completely new and different existence."

John Houston has a vision which he couldn't quite believe at the time.

> I still can't believe it. I do our shopping as a rule and I go down to Savacentre on Saturday mornings, usually early. And there was Robin pushing the cart, with one kid sitting up and the other kid lying in another bit, and Robin had a great big fluffy toy creature he'd just bought for them… and, well, the idea of seeing Robin, the Robin Philipson I knew, with these two kids and a trolley of groceries… it was something else. I just burst out laughing. He was at the next checkout, saw me, smiled, and said "I know."

Philipson and the man who was very much his opposite number in Glasgow, the legendary David Donaldson, former head of painting at Glasgow School of Art and the Queen's Limner in Scotland, reached their "three score and ten" in the same year, 1986. If, in the eyes of many people, Philipson epitomised the urbane and gracious ambassador for Scottish art, Donaldson, in his own cultivated way, represents what you might expect from the doyen of Glasgow painters – earthy, often outrageous and, in Glasgow's own word for it, "gallus." The two men joshed each other frequently, but beyond the repartee enjoyed the most sincere mutual respect. It was a happy thought by The Fine Art Society to honour their seventieth birthday year with complementary exhibitions which opened in their own cities then transferred to the other. Donaldson included in his show the portrait of Philipson, commissioned by the RSA. He also underlined the image of himself as a Glaswegian, which he cultivates so assiduously, by revealing a self-portrait *Myself at 70* with an emblematic fish supper in his hands.

Philipson's contribution to the joint birthday celebration, which ran into the early months of 1987, was symphonic in scale and in the way it gathered up some of his familiar thematic statements and reiterated them with fresh impetus in dramatic new compositions. The exhibition was dominated by two big theatrical triptychs *The Trap* and *Ho! Ho! the Hobby Horse* – each of which has references to the French Revolution – and many studies made on the way to the finished works. For three days, chittering in the bitter cold of the abattoir, he had sketched animal carcases at Gorgie slaughterhouse. "Later," he recalled, "going through the wardrobe of clothes I keep for dressing-up – party costume for myself, or for a studio mock-up – I came across a handsome coat [his favourite item of "revels" apparel?], probably seventeenth or eighteenth century. I don't know why, but for some reason I saw these Gorgie carcases wearing this coat, and variations of it, on a fairground roundabout."

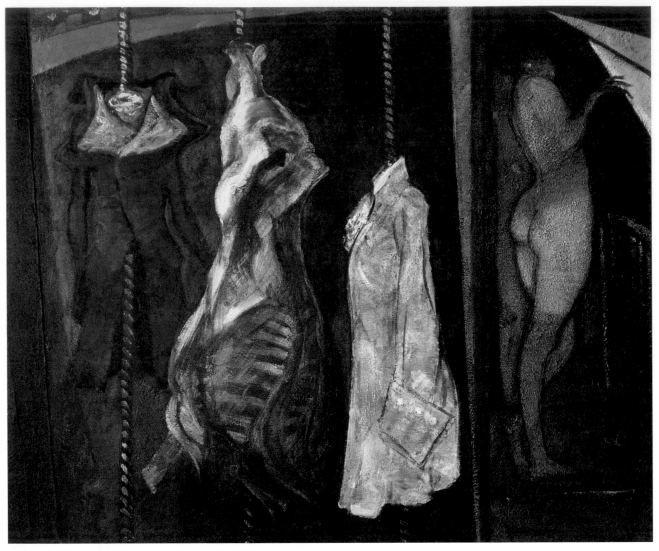

The ox-carcases are at the heart of both triptychs. In *The Trap* they occupy the centre panel – a brave charcoal homage to Rembrandt – flanked by women ascending one of life's ladders and a snake descending another. In the left-hand panel a painting of fierce snarling dogs sits on a studio easel. In the right-hand panel the easel casts the image of a guillotine and a cross; dead dogs lie on the floor, a cocked hat floats above a military greatcoat and beneath a frieze of naked women.

The sombre tones of *The Trap* give way to grislier colour in *Ho! Ho! the Hobby Horse*, garish in its fairground vulgarity. The horses go nowhere at a frenzied gallop, the dead meat draped in the coats is skewered on the carousel's vertical rods, naked women and soldiers joyride to perdition, and a headsman leans pensively on his axe. Many other paintings in the exhibition – *The Same Old Game*, *Arena* and its sixteen studies of noble horses and horsemanship, another triptych *Classical Studies* and haunting small mysteries like The *Beckoning* and *The Visit – Night* spoke of new energies and increased appetites. He was more open than ever to the spiritual and physical peradventure which fuelled his impatient mind.

"Ho! Ho! The Hobby Horse"

"The Same Old Game"

"Ho! Ho! The Hobby Horse"

"Ho! Ho! The Hobby Horse"

Later in 1987 the birth of a son, Anthony, to Robin and Diana Philipson, a joyful addition to a happy family, was overshadowed when a recurrence of the cancer which had laid him low at Boulogne sent him once more to the operating theatre. Even before the boy was born it had become obvious that the presence of three small children would make painting at home almost impossible. Good friends made a commodious nearby flat available to him on generous terms, but it was some time before he felt fit enough to take up their offer. When he did, he enjoyed the independence of the first studio he had ever occupied which was not tied to college or home. He came and went when he wanted to, encouraged a small circle of intimate friends to call on him, and began work for a second exhibition at the Bruton Gallery in Somerset. After donating a painting called *The Secret Garden* to a charity in celebration of Glasgow's 1988 Garden Festival the subject began to burgeon into a theme.

> I found myself enmeshed in circumstances of daydreaming that seemed to be timeless, and first place was given to that association of ideas and images sprung from the shadowed depths of consciousness rather than the illuminated world of logic. *The Secret Garden* became as it is, I think, for everyone, an attitude of mind: for me a recapitulation of old and favourite images – the zebra, the cattle, the irony of ladies and the fickleness of light. Through this evocation of timelessness drifted symbols of the rose window, the fighting cocks and fish with, for me, their secret overtones of association.

At the end of the year he needed the first of several remedial operations to remove adhesions and a hernia, but was spirited enough to tell a journalist: "I haven't been lucky, but I don't think about it. I just get on with life. I can't see why I shouldn't be like my parents and live into my nineties."

The spring and summer of 1989 were taken up with elaborate preparations for an Edinburgh Festival retrospective – the biggest and most comprehensive show of Philipson's work ever mounted. The venue was Edinburgh College of Art. In the 40 years of his professional career he had sold many hundreds of paintings and drawings. He had been less than precise in naming and dating his work, especially the thematic subjects, and the exact whereabouts of some of his most important paintings was unknown. The awesome task of tracking them down, selecting the best, organising the exhibition, planning its presentation and collaborating with the artist's wishes fell to his friend Colin Thomson, former director of the National Gallery of Scotland. There were over 150 catalogued exhibits – perhaps, in hindsight, 50 too many. They spanned all the years between the Kokoschka-inspired *Summer Morning* and Brenda's spring portrait and the first of a new and important blossoming of poppies.

Exhausted by the labour and excitement of the retrospective he nevertheless settled down to make fresh experiments with the use of abstraction to define and allocate pictorial space, to address the canvas with a more improvisatory attitude, but – above all – to perfect a technique of underpainting and glazing which would make very large paintings of poppies one of the achievements of his artistic lifetime.

> What attracted me to poppies was their splendour – the sheer power and yet the delicacy of their colour – the cold and warm reds and very subtle translucent lights.
>
> I began by modelling their form in whites and a range of neutral colours. When this "white" stage was quite dry, the strong colours were created by laying thin glazes of pale transparent paint over the top, sometimes up to ten or more one on top of the other. Some of the blacks are built up in the same way over a bed of very rich blue or crimson.
>
> Working with glazes means that design and colour scheme have to be planned in advance, the forms themselves have to be more precisely determined – effects cannot be produced directly as they can in painting straight on to the canvas.

A 1990 show of these shimmering, gorgeous blooms – voluptuous and blowsy, delicate and vulnerable – many of them painted on canvases six feet by four feet, turned the Fine Art Society's galleries in Glasgow and Edinburgh into radiant bowers. I wrote at the time that I felt it necessary to close the gallery door very carefully behind me in case a sudden draught brought their petals tumbling to the floor.

His old pal Bill Baillie saw many of these poppies on their way to full bloom and recalls how their serenity was captured in a tempest of activity.

> He worked himself to a frazzle in that studio in the last days. Day after day after day, and nights too. His main concern was the family. He wanted not so much to sell pictures for the sake of selling pictures, but making them, taking on commissions, to leave a secure basis for the family. He knew the score. He often said to me, "It's sad that I won't see them in their teens." That was just a recognised thing with him, poor man.

Twice more during a year in which, ironically, he was made an honorary Fellow of the Royal College of Surgeons, he was again under the knife. Every operation took its toll and extended the time he needed for recovery. Glasgow paid its respects to him in its celebrations as 1990 European City of Culture with another honorary university degree: the *matière* artists Antoni Tapies and Alberto Burri, architect James Stirling, poet Edwin Morgan and singer Elisabeth Schwarzkopf were honoured the same day.

By 1991 he was becoming more and more physically depleted, but the drying time of successive glazed poppy canvases allowed him to patch in a little colour here, reveal more light there. Many of what turned out to be his final sequence of poppy paintings were for valuable commissions which he felt unable to refuse. All his romantic sensitivity and exquisite craft skills went into the decoration of wooden chests – *Fruit Box* and *Sea Chest* – for the family who owned his studio. And still he grappled with ideas, wrestled with fresh approaches to painting design. Among many watercolours he made direct homage to past masters Daguerre and Daumier, re-interpreted *The Judgement of Paris* in pastels, and worked on a large oil, costumed partygoers in tumbling abandon with a wan portrait of himself, "the chield amang you taking notes," in the bottom right-hand corner. He called it *Zigzag of Time* and it became the title of his last show – at the Bruton Gallery, Bath.

"Sir Robin Philipson" by Jack Firth
(Scottish National Portrait Gallery)

He collapsed during the private view in November 1991 and, back in Edinburgh, underwent another major operation. For some weeks in 1992 he struggled to the studio and did what he could. Standing at the easel became too much for him so he concentrated on watercolours and pastels. By the time he started a course of chemotherapy even gentle sketching sitting by the fire at home was beyond him.

> You don't know where the hell you're going, anyway. You paint within an orbit of lack of definition, lack of orientation often, and just lack of sheer knowledge of what this great great job is all about. As you get older, happily, you don't care a tuppeny damn. You're really rather glad that you don't have to care about where you're going. You're more deeply puzzled, of course, and I suggest that this is the right and proper attitude, because we don't know too much of the mysteries of the world. You can speculate in your work about that infinity which we're going to approach relatively soon, and that might turn out to be, you hope, an enlightening of the mystery to other people. But that's no damn use to you, whatsoever. That's about it…

POSTSCRIPT

OUR LAST MEETING, IN THE EARLY EVENING OF APRIL 13, 1992, WAS IN the big front room at Crawfurd Road. It had been a girny, dull day. He had been too ill to see me for a few weeks. I was shocked to find him frail to the point of being almost transparent, happed in a blanket, clutching a hot water bottle to his belly. My wine was airing, as usual, by the fire. His eyes, sunken in that handsome, curiously square head, flashed with fires that he managed to summon from somewhere. The room had been redecorated, the better to accommodate an enormous and majestic John Bellany flower painting which hung in a wall recess behind him and dwarfed his wasted, diminutive figure. Out of that traditional affection that some artists have for each other, master and former pupil had swapped paintings. It slumbered on the wall behind him as he ranged, with extraordinary vivacity, through the themes of his painting life, recapitulating what they had meant to him, musing over what they might have meant to others. Despite his determination to go on covering as much ground as he could, I think we both knew that this roll-call might be the last. He was tiring fast. The westering sun suddenly pierced the clouds and a spear of light hit Bellany's flowers. The whole room was bathed in their radiance, and Robin, oblivious to a suffusion of colour that might have come from one of his own rose windows, talked about the music he played while working at the easel.

At Robin's funeral only a few weeks later our mutual friend Tom Fleming met me outside the church and asked how I was. "Fine." "Are you sure?" He gave me a long anxious look. That afternoon, going round the RSA summer show, I felt very peculiar. Within 24 hours I had an emergency blood transfusion. Within a fortnight I was on the operating table undergoing major colonic surgery.

I was convalescing at home and missed the opening of a big Bellany restrospective show in Glasgow. When John and Helen arrived back in Edinburgh from the private view they came straight to my door with a gift – the magnificent bouquet, an armful of flowers cunningly arranged to echo Bellany's vibrant palette, which Glasgow Art Galleries had presented to Helen. I stood the flowers with the sun at their backs and for many days watched this symbolic requiem glow and resonate, come the full circle, until the flowers hung their heads.

BRIEF CHRONOLOGY

1916   Born, December 17, at Broughton Mills, Cumbria.

1930   Family moved to Gretna. Educated at Dumfries Academy

1936   Edinburgh College of Art

1940   DA (Edin)

1940–46 War service with King's Own Scottish Borderers, commissioned to Royal Indian Army Service Corps, served in India and Burma.

1946   Teacher training at Moray House, Edinburgh.

1947   Following temporary post as assistant librarian became lecturer in drawing and painting.

1948   Elected professional member of SSA

1949   Married Brenda Mark

1951   Guthrie Award at RSA for "Spring Portrait – Brenda"

1952   Elected ARSA. First "Fighting Cocks."

1954   First solo exhibition – the Scottish Gallery. Living in West Bow, Edinburgh.

1955   Elected RSW

1956   Painted "View of Princes Street" (Walker Art Gallery, Liverpool)

1957   Visited Paris to select works for RSA loan exhibition.

1958   Second Scottish Gallery show. Designed poster for Edinburgh Festival.

1959   Third prize in John Moores Biennial.

1960   Death of Brenda Philipson. Succeeds William Gillies as Head of Drawing and Painting, ECA. First London solo show – at Roland, Browse and Delbanco. Painted "The Burning."

1961   Second London show. Married Thora Clyne.

1962   Elected RSA

1963   Visiting Professor of Painting, University of Colorado.

1964   First major illness. Visited Warsaw.

1965   Edinburgh Festival exhibition. "Stone the Crows." "Defenders of the Realm," other war paintings.

1966   Glasgow Airport mural

1967   Cargill Award at RGI

1968   Altarpieces, the arrival of "Waiting Women" and "Women Observed."

1969   Elected Secretary of RSA, member of Edinburgh Festival Council. Work shown in New York.

1970   Scottish Arts Council touring exhibition "Cockfight and Rosewindow." Dunfermline retrospective.

1971   30-minute film profile Scope for BBC television

1972   Sabbatical – interrupted by major illness at Boulogne.

1973   Elected ARA. Elected President of the RSA

1974   Exhibitions at Elgin and Haddington. Mexican altars, church interiors, zebra paintings.

1975   Divorced. Visited Belgrade.

1976   Married Diana Pollock. Knighted for services to the arts in Scotland. More awards and distinctions. Scholarships for travel in Kenya and South Africa. Dog paintings, herds of cattle, baboons.

1977   Mural for Dundee College of Education. Stirling retrospective.

1978   Elected FRSE. Aberdeen LL.D.

1979   Stirling Gallery exhibition

1980   Elected RGI, honorary RCAA. "Men Observed" and "Cardinal" paintings.

1981   Elected RA.

1982   Retired as head of school, ECA.

1983   Demitted office as PRSA. Major Edinburgh Festival exhibition.

1985   D.Univ. from Heriot-Watt University. Exhibition at Bruton Gallery, Somerset.

1986	Joint exhibition "At Seventy" with David Donaldson, Glasgow and Edinburgh. "Arena" paintings and various interpretations of the merry-go-round theme.
1987	Major surgery
1988	Year of major exhibitions, Edinburgh, Somerset, Wales, and more surgery.
1989	Huge retrospective exhibition during Edinburgh Fesitval at ECA.
1990	Large poppy paintings. D.Litt from Glasgow University. Made Hon Fellow of Royal College of Surgeons. Yet more surgery. Begins final series of "Poppies."
1991	Elected Hon RWA. Returns to small watercolours and pastels. Homage to Daguerre, Daumier, etc. "Zigzag of Time" exhibition, Bruton Gallery, Bath. Major surgery, November.
1992	Two months at studio before becoming too ill to work. Chemotherapy begun in April. Died, aged 75, Edinburgh Royal Infirmary, May 26.

EXHIBITIONS

Throughout his career Robin Philipson's work was in constant demand for important group exhibitions, alongside other contemporary artists, all over Britain and across the world. He is represented in many important international collections. The following is a list of his solo exhibitions in Britain, spanning almost 40 years.

1954	Scottish Gallery, Edinburgh
1958	Scottish Gallery, Edinburgh
1960	Roland, Browse and Delbanco, London
1961	Scottish Gallery, Edinburgh
1962	Roland, Browse and Delbanco, London
1964	Roland, Browse and Delbanco, London
1965	Scottish Gallery, Edinburgh. Festival Exhibition
1967	Roland, Browse and Delbanco, London
1968	Scottish Gallery, Edinburgh

1969	Loomshop Gallery, Lower Largo
1970	Scottish Gallery, Edinburgh
1970	Retrospective Exhibition – "Cockfight Rosewindow" Scottish Arts Council. Edinburgh
1970	Retrospective Exhibition. The Carnegie Trust, Dunfermline
1971	Roland, Browse and Delbanco, London
1973	Scottish Gallery, Edinburgh. "Boulogne and After"
1974	Exhibition of Cathedral Paintings, Elgin
1974	Lamp of Lothian, Haddington House. Edinburgh Festival Exhibition
1975	Roland, Browse and Delbanco, London
1976	Loomshop Gallery, Lower Largo. Scottish Gallery, Edinburgh. Festival Exhibition – Watercolours and Paintings
1977	Retrospective Exhibition, MacRobert Centre, University of Stirling
1978	Loomshop Gallery, Lower Largo
1978	Roland, Browse and Delbanco, London – "Women Observed"
1979	Stirling Gallery
1980	Macaulay Gallery, Stenton
1981	Browse and Darby Gallery, London
1982	Macaulay Gallery, Stenton. Loomshop Gallery, Lower Largo
1983	Scottish Gallery, Edinburgh – Festival Exhibition. English Speaking Union, Edinburgh. New Peter Potter Gallery, Haddington
1984	Browse and Darby Gallery, London
1985	Bruton Gallery, Somerset. "Exhibition of Recent Paintings". Loomshop Gallery, Lower Largo
1986/87	Fine Art Society, Edinburgh & Glasgow. "At Seventy – David Donaldson and Robin Philipson." Browse and Darby, London. Lamp of Lothian, Haddington

1988   Bruton Gallery, Somerset "The Secret Garden" Retrospective Exhibition, The Scottish Arts Club, Edinburgh

1989   Major Retrospective Exhibition, Edinburgh College of Art

1990   Fine Art Society, Edinburgh & Glasgow

1991   Bruton Gallery, Bath. Inaugural exhibition

1992   Posthumous Exhibition to mark 25 years of the Lamp of Lothian at Haddington House.

HONOURS and AWARDS

1952   ARSA

1955   RSW

1961   RSA

1965   FRSA

1973   PRSA
       ARA

1974   HRA

1976   KNIGHTHOOD
       Commandeur de l'Ordre du Mérite de la République Française
       Hon. Doctorate of University of Stirling

1978   LL. D (Aberdeen)
       FRSE

1980   RGI
       HRHA
       RCAA

1981   RA

1983   Hon. FRIAS

1985   Hon. Doctorate of Heriot-Watt University

1990   Hon. FRCS, Edinburgh
       D. Litt. Glasgow University

1991   RWA

ABBREVIATIONS

NGS   National Galleries of Scotland

SNPG   Scottish National Portrait Gallery

SNGMA   Scottish National Gallery of Modern Art

RSA   Royal Scottish Academy

RA   Royal Academician

RSW   Royal Scottish Society of Painters in Water-colours

SSA   Society of Scottish Artists

RGI   Royal Glasgow Institute of the Fine Arts

FRSE   Fellow of the Royal Society of Edinburgh

HFHA   Hon Fellow of Hibernian Academy

RCAA   Fellow of Royal Canadian Academy of Arts

HFRIAS   Hon Fellow of Royal Incorporation of Architects in Scotland

RWA   Royal West of England Academician

FRCS   Hon Fellow Royal College of Surgeons

INDEX

BUMPUS, Judith

BUSBY, John

CALLENDER, Robert

CLYNE, Thora

CONVERY, Francis

CROSBIE, William

CROZIER, William

CUMMING, James

DAVIE, Alan

DELBANCO, Gustave

DONALDSON, David

EARDLEY, Joan

EVANS, David

FENTON, FW

FIRTH, Jack

FLEMING, Ian

FLEMING, Tom

GAGE, Edward

GILLIES, William

GWILLIAM, Phyllis

HALL, Douglas

HARDIE, William

HOFFMAN, Edith

HOUSTON, John

HOWISON, Charlie

KEOWN, Eric

KNOX, Jack

KOKOSCHKA, Oskar

LINDSAY, Maurice

LOCHHEAD, Tom

McLELLAN, Sadie

McCLURE, David & Joyce

MACMILLAN, Duncan

MACMILLAN, Very Rev G.

MACTAGGART, William

MARK, Brenda

MAXWELL, John

MICHIE, David

MOFFAT, Sandy

MORRIS, Desmond

MORRISON, James

MORROCCO, Alberto

MULLALY, Terence

NEWTON, Eric

PEPLOE, Denis

PEPLOE, Guy

PEPLOE, S. J.

PHILIPSON, James

PHILIPSON, John

POLLOCK, Diana

POSTLETHWAITE, Agnes

RAMSAY, Jock

REDFERN, June

REDPATH, Anne

THOMSON, Colin

WALKER, Frances

WELLINGTON, Hubert

WESTWATER, "Peter"

WHEELER, Sir Anthony

WILSON, William